FOAL

SEEING LIFE THROUGH PRIVATE EYES

Secrets from America's Top Investigator to Living Safer, Smarter, and Saner

Thomas G. Martin

ROWMAN & LITTLEFIELD
Lanham • Boulder • New York • London

Published by Rowman & Littlefield
A wholly owned subsidary of
The Rowman & Littlefield Publishing Group, Inc.
4501 Forbes Boulevard, Suite 200, Lanham, Maryland 20706
https://rowman.com

Unit A, Whitacre Mews, 26-34 Stannary Street, London SE11 4AB,
United Kingdom

British Library Cataloguing in Publication Information Available

Library of Congress Cataloging-in-Publication Data
Names: Martin, Thomas G., 1946– author.
Title: Seeing life through private eyes : secrets from America's top investigator
    to living safer, smarter, and saner / Thomas G. Martin.
Description: Lanham : Rowman & Littlefield, [2017] | Includes index.
Identifiers: LCCN 2016057281 (print) | LCCN 2017014210 (ebook) | ISBN
    9781442269736 (electronic) | ISBN 9781442269729 (cloth : alk. paper)
Subjects: LCSH: Martin, Thomas G., 1946- | Private investigators—United
    States—Biography. | Crime prevention—United States.
Classification: LCC HV8083.M276 (ebook) | LCC HV8083.M276 A3 2017
    (print) | DDC 363.28/9092 [B] —dc23
LC record available athttps://lccn.loc.gov/2016057281

∞ ™ The paper used in this publication meets the minimum requirements of
American National Standard for Information Sciences Permanence of Paper
for Printed Library Materials, ANSI/NISO Z39.48-1992.

Printed in the United States of America

To our grandchildren: Trevor, Derek, Julia, Shane, Claire, and Graham

Know that you are all unique, beautiful, wanted, and irreplaceable. Your grandmother Martin and I love you dearly. Remember, when you are away from us physically, you are always in our hearts.

Some say life is a sprint, others a marathon. As grandparents, we like to believe it is more like a relay race, one in which we are hopefully passing batons spiritually, physically, mentally, and academically to you in your young lives. Use them to be happy but also to help those less fortunate. Now is the time for us to invest in your future. Be bold and return the favor later in life to others.

CONTENTS

ACKNOWLEDGMENTS

My heartfelt gratitude and sincere thanks to the following people whose efforts contributed to the completion of this book:

Mike Garroutte—Loyal, street-smart, diligent, and patient. At my side for thirty-five years, he worked almost all of the cases in this book. From my chair, he is one of the top private investigators in America.

Brian Chernicky—The "originator" of the idea for me to write this book. Internet marketing specialist with no peer in the industry; thinks outside of the box with no fluff or spin. Totally responsible for the title of this book.

Paula Miller—For thirty years, my administrative assistant who has overseen and maintained the excellence of our agency's reports. She single-handedly ensured accuracy and clarity when those reports were submitted to judges and/or juries.

Julie McCarron—An exceptional editor and even better person. Knowledgeable, thorough, and ever willing to make the product first-rate. I will be ever grateful for her consistent temperament and contagious enthusiasm for giving the reader our best effort.

Kathryn Knigge—As our main contact at Rowman & Littlefield, she brought character, calmness, and guidance throughout the entire process. Her pleasant demeanor was complemented by a literary guiding hand that was purposeful and enlightening.

BizMSolutions—We are grateful to Janice Clark for providing us with ongoing support of our online marketing efforts and access to her innovative team of social media marketing professionals. We are thankful for her invaluable guidance and friendly advice.

INTRODUCTION

As an ambitious young agent in the Bureau of Narcotics and Danger-ous Drugs (BNDD) in the late sixties, I was gung ho about America's newly declared "War on Drugs." Early on I set my sights high and decided I was going to become the number-two guy in the entire agen-cy. Of the two top positions on the BNDD food chain, number one is an administrator chosen by the president. The number-two spot is the deputy administrator. I'm not sure I would have had the political moxie to ever reach my lofty goal, but I got off to a strong start. I was on the career fast track as I was quickly promoted through all the government job levels: GS-7, GS-9, GS-11, GS-12, and GS-13, becoming a GS-14 agent in near-record time. Only one other agent—the man who pro-moted me—had climbed the ladder so quickly.

In the BNDD and subsequent Drug Enforcement Administration (DEA), which was established in 1973, there is only one philosophy: Get it done. Kick ass; take names; do whatever it takes. Like serving arrest and search warrants and going through doors without a clue who might be on the other side. The work we did was dangerous and punish-ing, but I never questioned that we were doing the right things for the right reasons and making a difference for good in the world. I was a true believer. I did things by the book. I never deviated from my mission, always followed the rules, and ensured my reputation was above re-proach.

My last assignment was supposed to be Florida—my new position a direct stepping-stone to headquarters in Washington, DC, and my ultimate goal. My wife and I had already bought a house there when a leg injury forced me out of service. I did not want to leave, but the DEA physician and my own doctor both insisted the damage was a career-ender, and it was. I would never become deputy administrator. The loss of my job was devastating, and I was melancholy about "what could have been" for several weeks. Staying home with my two young children brought me back to reality, quickly. I needed to find another career.

Thirty-six years later, I know my forced retirement was the best thing that ever happened to me. As a government agent I made some major busts and put away some highly dangerous individuals, which certainly saved a few lives somewhere. Still, any impact I might have had as a BNDD/DEA agent doesn't come close to what I have accomplished in over three decades as a private investigator. In this job, I change lives every day—and it's easy to judge my results. I get the guy out of jail or I don't. I find all the missing assets or I don't, nail that cheating spouse, crack the cold case . . . or I don't. There's not a whole lot of gray in this job.

Mainly because of all the movies, television shows, and books starring private eyes, most people have a not-entirely accurate perception of what private eyes do. Here is what you need to know: a top-notch investigator is your best friend in all kinds of situations. He (or she) is trained to solve the mysteries, uncover the problem, and correct misdeeds in a way that keeps you safe, doesn't waste your time, money, or energy, and gets the job done efficiently. You regain your peace of mind and move on with your life!

I always tell people that it's better to know me and not need me . . . than to need me and not know me. In this book you will get to know me, America's PI. "Me" meaning not just myself, but some of the other absolute top experts in the business from Martin Investigative Services. I will share some stories from my BNDD/DEA days and talk about some of my more memorable cases from my thirty-five years as a top PI. I want you to see the world the way I see it, so you'll be better able to prepare for and protect yourself from life's inevitable pitfalls.

In short, I want to give you what the very best investigators deliver: safety, security, knowledge, and peace of mind. I hope you find the answers you are seeking in the pages ahead.

I

THE LIFE OF A PI

The general public has all kinds of preconceived notions about private investigators. This has much to do with the way they have been portrayed in television shows and movies through the years. Early on, Sam Spade and Philip Marlowe epitomized the "hard-boiled" detective immortalized by Humphrey Bogart onscreen; at the other end of the spectrum Tom Selleck wisecracked his way through Hawaii on *Magnum, PI*, in the 1980s. The reality, of course, is quite different. For those who are interested in actually making a living in this profession, let me share with you some hard-won lessons.

In the early eighties, after I left the DEA, I rented a tiny one-room office where I shared a receptionist and conference room with the other tenants. Old habits died hard. Every morning I dressed in a suit and tie, as I always had while working as a supervisor for the government. I'd head to the office, sit at my desk, listen to the radio, read the paper. At night, I'd return home and take off my suit. My wife snapped at me one morning when I put on the same shirt again for the second day in a row. Why not? I protested. I was sitting quietly all day . . . I wasn't running around getting my hands dirty! I wasn't doing much at all, to be honest.

The hazy plan I had was to find some clients in the general public and hopefully build my business through word of mouth. The Yellow Pages had no ads for any firms or agencies, but there were a number of male names listed under "Private Investigators." On a couple of those days as I sat in my office with a phone that didn't ring, an empty

Rolodex, and no visitors or clients, I cold-called the names in the phone book. I introduced myself and said that I was setting up shop as a PI. I asked where their office was located and about the state of business. Not one person I spoke to had an office; they all worked out of their homes. Most were retired law enforcement officers who picked up "investigation" jobs from the county.

I learned that many of these "PIs" were working for seven or eight dollars an hour. This was a long time ago, of course, but still. The only skill required for those with private clients, it seemed to me, was the ability to follow people around to see if they were cheating on someone. The luckier ones were hired by the county for the plum workmen's comp cases at ten dollars an hour. Again, this was about following people around, in these cases to see if they truly did have a bad back. The county was really squeezing these people . . . to a level I considered downright abusive. If that was the best money I could make as a PI, I'd find something else to do.

After a couple weeks of sitting in the empty office, I got a little desperate. Something needed to happen. So I approached the editors at major area newspapers and told them that if their reporters were working on any big stories, I would do the background investigations on the people or companies involved for free. I went to the local television stations and made the same offer. They all looked at me like I was crazy, and pretty much shooed me out the door, but then something broke.

"I came across this case," a reporter I knew one day said. "The guy's been convicted of rape—wrongly, he says. He has some money, and he's hell-bent on getting another trial. Do you want to take a look?"

I was happy to take a look; I wasn't exactly busy. I went to the courthouse and got a transcript of the trial. The short story was that a man I will call James Royce had been involved in a bitter divorce. His wife, who happened to be the head of the local Chamber of Commerce, accused him of sexually abusing her teenage daughter during the marriage. The teenage girl, Tami, swore that her stepfather had been molesting her for years. A county district attorney had made this his pet case and splashed lurid details all over the press during the long trial. In the end, Royce was convicted of sexual abuse of a minor and was currently waiting to be sentenced.

I read every page of the transcript through carefully before I met with James in person. When I met him, I cut right to the chase. "Dude, you're guilty. You are going to go to prison. There is nothing I can do for you."

"I did not touch that girl," he swore. I'd heard protestations of innocence before a thousand times when I was a DEA agent, so his declaration didn't move me in the slightest. The only reason I took the case was that I had absolutely nothing else to do. He had some money, and I had some time. I think I charged him a grand total of something like five hundred dollars. I thought his request was such a complete waste of money that I didn't want to take more. I had plenty of faith in my own snap conclusions. I was smart and highly experienced, and I'd read that transcript with an eagle eye. The man was clearly guilty as hell.

But still . . . a case was a case. I set out to investigate, meaning interviewing or reinterviewing anyone affiliated in any way with this case. Legally, I was not allowed to speak to the girl or her mother. In the court of public opinion, my client was already dead and buried, given his very public conviction. Still, I persevered. By nosing around, I found an aunt, the mother's sister, who had at one point been close to her niece. "I've got a bunch of Tami's stuff she left at my house you can have . . . mostly clothes," she offered. I wasn't sure what I could determine from a bunch of girl's clothes, but thought I should probably at least take a quick look.

"Anything else in there?" I asked.

"A couple of books, textbooks . . . oh, and I think there's a diary."

That got my attention; I was very anxious indeed to read this teenage girl's uncensored thoughts. I collected the material and pored over the girlish handwriting in the cheap leather-covered diary. Right there, dated August 1978, when she would have been sixteen years old, were the words, "Gary devirginized me tonight." I had never heard that term, so I checked with my wife just to be sure. "That's what devirginized means, right, that it was the first time she'd ever had sex?"

"Of course, duh, yeah . . . and you're calling yourself an investigator?" my wife asked.

"Well, if this diary entry is true, then her stepfather James could not have been having sex with her months earlier!" I became very energized and started reaching out aggressively, looking for anyone at all related to the case far and wide. I found a marine in Washington State who had casually dated Tami. He came right out and told me, "Oh, those accusations were all just made up. It was a story she and her mom cooked up to really squeeze him and get more money in the divorce." I couldn't believe how cavalier he was when talking about ruining a man's entire life.

Next, I turned to her best friend, who was on the list of original witnesses but was never called to trial. I interviewed her again. When I pressed her about her friend's activities, she looked at me sadly and said, "Yes Mr. Martin, this was all really wrong. I should have said something to somebody at the time. What's really bothering me is that district attorney. He had a photo of his wife sitting right there on his desk the whole time!"

"So what, most people have family photos like that in their office. I have one of my own wife on my desk. What's the big deal?"

"Well, he was sleeping with Tami throughout the whole trial!"

Oh my God. Now this was like throwing a lighted match into a pool of gasoline. The Department of Justice had trained us to first clean our own linen, so that's what I tried to do. I wrote up the entire report, complete with sworn statements and my devastating conclusions. I then found James a new attorney. I took the whole matter over to the district attorney's office. "I've got two things to tell you," I said. "One, my client James Royce never touched his stepdaughter. He was set up. He wants a new trial, and he's going to get a new trial. The reason why is in here," I placed the report on his desk. "Second, you've got a really bad apple in your office here. You need to do something about him, fast."

A few weeks later, much to my disappointment, absolutely nothing had happened. No one ever called me, no one reached out to James or his new attorney. There was not one peep from the DA's office. So I called a press conference. I was a nobody, of course, no longer a hotshot DEA agent, so no one bothered to attend. Except for one young female reporter from KFWB radio. She broke the exclusive story later that week. The rest, as they say, was history.

I didn't have time to follow everything that happened after that, because I suddenly got very busy. I am pretty sure that particular DA wound up losing his law license . . . though in California you can do some pretty crazy stuff and still manage to get your license back. Up until a few years ago, Jimmy would send me Christmas cards and thank-you cards. He was never retried. My very first case was valuable in a number of ways—not least in which it was a much-needed reminder to approach every case with an open mind and leave my assumptions at the door!

* * *

There are four main areas of business for a private investigator: working for private clients, for attorneys, for corporations, and for insurance companies. Working with the general public is not to every investigator's taste. It involves so much personal interaction and handling of messy emotions. Frankly, it's draining—I liken it to having twenty wives and fifteen kids you're babysitting . . . all at once! Many men aren't temperamentally cut out to handle marital issues. I don't know that I was particularly cut out for it either. However, when I started my business, I had no clients. I did have two young kids at home, so I was going to take anything that came my way. To this day, I credit the sensitivity and personal touch we developed with female clients for our great success in that area.

After the publicity I received from the James Royce case, my office was flooded with inquiries from the public. I had been in business for a good three years when it dawned on me: Maybe we should try to get some corporate clients. My thought was to do employment background checks. During the nineties, I shifted most of my workload to attorneys, corporations, and insurance companies. This was a simple matter of finances; individuals simply cannot pay the fees that a huge company can. Handling investigations in the business and legal arenas proved highly lucrative, though we remained a full-service agency.

The vast majority of top-tier PIs specialize in one genre or another. Many of the guys and gals who come from the federal agencies have mastered particular skills, spent years working in a certain area, and only want to deal with certain matters. Some just want to consult on white-collar crime. Some are experts on surveillance. Some only handle workers comp issues, and so on and so forth. It's great to have a particular area of expertise, but it can also lead to trouble.

My career as a private investigator started as a one-man show. At its high point, Martin Investigative was using forty-five people. This growth spurt came after a long period of holding steady with ten solid guys working for me as investigators. When business started to boom, I jumped in and added fifteen more for a total of twenty-five spread over offices all over California. I could afford to pay more by that time, and I cherry-picked the best of former Justice and Treasury Department workers. These guys and gals were all world-class; I had a great team in place.

But my next expansion, up to forty employees? I was scraping the barrel a little bit, to be honest. And those last five employees? Slim pickings. Frankly, I was having a hard time just finding forty-five quality people with their PI licenses current and in good standing in the Southern California area. I came to realize that one of three factors derailed even the most naturally talented investigators.

Specialization. I know plenty of great investigators who specialize in one particular area. If you are the best of the best, that's great. My technical surveillance expert, for example, couldn't conduct an interview to save his life. However, he is an absolute genius when it comes to debugging, bug sweeps, and/or electronic eavesdropping detection sweeps. Because he's that good, he stays busy and makes a great living. This can be a problem for the many other PIs who get stuck in one lane. They start out in stall number 7—insurance fraud, let's say—and stay there for the whole race.

I have always been, by necessity, a full-service guy. I constantly urge flexibility and solid all-around experience in all aspects of private investigation, with interview and interrogation always key. I am someone who started in the days when fax machines were state of the art. Now I'm keenly aware of the huge role social media plays in our investigations. I demand it of myself, and I encourage it in others: Be flexible. Continue to learn. Keep moving and changing and growing!

Big Ups, Big Downs. Every state has a different licensing system to officially qualify as a private investigator. With more than 100,000 PIs in the country today, obviously the problem is not getting licensed. The problem that trips up even brilliant investigators is the reality that being a PI is not a steady job. There are huge peaks and valleys. If you can accept that reality and survive the lean times, you can thrive. But too many people are buying a Mercedes one month and can't afford to put gas in its tank the next.

Many private investigators are former cops or agents, used to being "on the dole," also known as getting that steady government paycheck. There is no steady paycheck working for yourself, and there is no rhyme or reason to this business. You never know what will happen. In my early years, I assumed January would be slow because everyone was recovering from the holidays; February would be busy because of Valentine's Day; March would be busy with the blooming of spring . . . I had all kinds of models and projections that just never panned out. What I finally realized is that a PI is always just one phone call away from a big case.

One might also put that another way: in this business, you're always just a day away from bankruptcy. People used to laugh at me because I drove my original Mercedes for seventeen years. Everyone used to ask, "Why don't you get a nice car?"

"This is a nice car," I would reply. "It gets me where I need to go." I was nothing if not prudent. I rode out the big ups and downs of my early years in business. I saw too many other guys fail because they simply couldn't manage the downtimes. It was years and years before I finally bought a brand-new Mercedes SL. Not two weeks later, I went to interview with an entrepreneur who owned a fleet of garbage trucks. He had hundreds of them servicing routes all over LA County.

He also had a real problem with guys drinking on the job. Toward the end of the routes, many of the teams would stop by a 7-Eleven or supermarket, get a six-pack of beer, and drink it while they finished up their route for the day. Some drove their garbage trucks into an area known for drug dealing and made buys in the company vehicles. These were infractions that could have very serious repercussions for his business. He needed a full-scale investigation, fast.

"You're the third private eye I've seen," the owner said when I was ushered into his office. "I like to keep my interviews short. Show me what kind of car you drive." I hadn't been in the room ten seconds; we turned around and walked back outside into the parking lot, where he circled my brand-new car, peering closely into the windows. He stopped when he saw the temporary dealer plates—it was that new. "This is yours, right, not a rental?" he asked. He was a suspicious guy. He had to be, in his line of work.

"It's all mine, just bought it," I assured him. "Papers in the glovebox."

"You're hired." This man valued appearances; he figured if I had a beautiful expensive new car, then I was doing well. Therefore, I was the right man for him. The funny thing was that after all my years of preaching frugality and proudly driving my old car around this was the one and only time anything like this ever happened. It was also the one and only time it mattered. He remained a great client for more than ten years.

Hustle. My office suitemates in those early days used to look at me a bit strangely when I arrived in a suit and tie every day. They could clearly see no one came to consult me; I had no visible business taking me out of the office, and the phone never rang. Still, I had the discipline to keep office hours and dress like I had clients coming in. Someday, I knew, there would be clients, and I would be ready for them. There were others out there who were more talented than I was, for sure. But nobody wanted to work as hard as I did.

From that day to this, I wake up every day and work like it's a real possibility that I could lose the house today . . . even though that's no longer a valid concern. So many PIs have retired after a full twenty or thirty years in law enforcement and are really only looking to keep a hand in part-time. They want to allow plenty of time for golf. I personally don't golf, and my wife doesn't want me hanging around the house, so I'm still out there hustling every day. I've still got the fire in my belly . . . every world-class private eye should too.

* * *

One of the routine tasks private eyes often take on is what is commonly known as "serving papers." The technical term is "service of process"— the procedure where a person or business in a lawsuit is given appropriate written notice of legal action being taken. I was frequently called upon to serve these documents for civil and family law matters, a job I did myself when I was a one-man show. These days I leave it to junior associates. While it is often a very mundane and/or boring process, it is not without its dangers. All investigators—and process servers—need to be continuously vigilant.

As a rule, no one is ever pleased to be served. We have been run off many properties by an irate, soon-to-be ex-husband or a plate-throwing, out-of-control mother who just found out the court wants to take her children away. Years ago, I gave a brand-new investigator in our office the fairly easy task of serving an eighty-two-year-old female who refused to either pay rent or vacate the premises. Eager to make a good impression on his first assignment, he bounded across the yard, crossed the porch, and rapped authoritatively on the door. He was greeted by a tiny lady with a big smile and a .38 Smith & Wesson 6-shot revolver pointed directly at his nose. He dropped the paper and fled. (It was deemed a good service by the court.)

Fortunately, although our investigators have served thousands of people papers over the years, no one has suffered any real bodily harm. Others are not so fortunate. Process servers have been killed when serving divorce papers and domestic injunctions. An enraged home-owner, believing he was being served a foreclosure notice, drove his backhoe into a process server's car, nearly beheading a child in the backseat. In a particularly grisly case in 2016, a female process server in Texas was attacked and killed by loose dogs while attempting to serve civil papers.

The very real issue of physical danger aside, getting people to come to their front door is a difficult task, especially if they know the papers are coming. One of the many ruses we use is purchasing a dozen red roses in a beautiful container. A knock on the front door is usually greeted by a female anxious to receive her special gift. On another process service, our same young investigator used this technique and came back to our corporate office very pleased with how smoothly service had been handled. Of course, he'd made what we considered a rookie mistake.

When I asked him where the roses were, he proudly related that he had handed them to the subject with the subpoena tucked neatly inside. He got a little red-faced when told that you never actually give the subject the flowers. You simply take the papers out of the arrangement, serve the subject, and give the roses to your wife. Lesson learned.

☼ ☼ ☼

The entertainment press frequently refers to "celebrity PIs" when re-porting on the latest movie star divorce or scandal. Particularly in cities like New York and Los Angeles, some investigators aspire to become "private eye to the stars." However, the skill set necessary to become a first-class investigator is exactly the same no matter who you work for. Stars have the same issues with kids and marriage and paying the bills as everyone else. The difference is simply a matter of scale—plus they've got a whole lot more people to help them.

Because Martin Investigative Services has been a presence in Los Angeles and Orange County for over three decades, we've picked up some celebrity clients along the way. Once high-profile people realize that we are not going to violate their confidence, we gain their trust and referrals to other friends and family members. I have more clients in the entertainment industry than any other PI in the country. But will you ever see me advertise as "PI to the Stars" or something like that? Never. I don't want that appellation. I would never violate the trust my clients place in my discretion.

In 1989, a beautiful young actress named Rebecca Schaeffer was shot point-blank and killed in her own West Hollywood doorway by an obsessed male fan who had been stalking her for three years. It turned out that her killer, Robert Bardo, had hired a private investigator in his hometown of Tucson to obtain her home address. He reportedly got the idea by reading a clipping about another actress, Theresa Saldana, whose stalker got her address this same way. Bardo's PI accessed Schaeffer's address through California's Department of Motor Vehicle records, which at that time were legally accessible to investigators.

Shock waves reverberated throughout California at this senseless murder. An immediate and intense campaign began to deter stalkers and strengthen privacy laws. California soon became the first state to pass anti-stalker legislation in 1990; other states quickly followed suit over the next few years. By 1994, the state's Driver's Privacy Protection Act (DPPA) prohibiting the disclosure of a driver's personal information was finally passed into law.

What all this meant for private investigators is that locating someone through driver's license records stopped pretty much the day Miss Schaeffer was murdered. These days, there are very, very few PIs with access to license plate or driver's license information. Having a PI license does not automatically grant access to that information; there is an extremely strict set of requirements that needs to be met to access such records. However, there are now so many other ways to obtain home addresses through many other sources: property records, Social Security records, billing records. Our own database contains all these and more.

Still, privacy concerns do not prevent the occasional person from calling to ask me if I can find Leonardo DiCaprio's address, for example. Now, this person might have a valid reason to want to reach out to him. They might want to send him a movie script, pass on a heartfelt fan request from a dying child, or who knows what. Whatever the story, my answer is no. I could find out where he lives, but that is not something I would take on. I felt that way long before 1989, and I still feel that way today. Everyone is entitled to his or her privacy.

Meanwhile, I just stay on the job. I go to court with celebrities. I testify for them and against them in divorce cases or employment matters. Sometimes I've been retained by the estranged husbands and wives of movie and sports stars, who then see my work up close and personal . . . and reach out to me themselves the next time. I am just as happy to work through their attorney, manager, or PA (personal assistant). I'm not a particularly star-struck kind of guy. I'm perfectly content to be a low-key member of the team.

Still, I will admit that sometimes it can all become a bit intoxicating. We are in a very unusual position vis-à-vis celebrities. For example, doing background checks for a huge footwear or beverage company, I've interviewed the most elite superstar athletes in the world. They are on the verge of being offered multi-million-dollar endorsement contracts, and the corporations have come to us to uncover the good, the bad, and the ugly. They want to know everything . . . *everything* . . . about their potential spokesperson, so there are no unpleasant surprises down the road.

We've got a standard list of a hundred or so questions we ask them. Not only, "When's the last time you had sex?" but "When's the last time you had sex without a condom?" and . . . "How many children do you have?" They often lie and embellish the truth. These people have been put on a pedestal all their lives, and they're surrounded by an entourage of yes-men. It's been years since anyone challenged a word they say. We do.

You have to have a strong internal moral compass when you're working in that kind of rarefied environment. Los Angeles "PI to the Stars" Anthony Pellicano ran completely off the rails. I met him back in the nineties, when he was making quite a name for himself with his hardball tactics in celebrity cases.

Like so many others mentioned throughout this book, Anthony thought he was too smart to get caught. He was wrong. He is currently serving fifteen years in federal prison for a host of offenses, including running a criminal enterprise. A number of LAPD officers, attorneys, and even a famous director went down with him.

Here's my final word on being a "celebrity PI": I once followed the model/actress/whatever wife of a very famous baseball player during their messy marital split. This was way back in the day when Howard Stern was the King of All Media and his radio show was required listening for everyone in Hollywood. She called me out by name while being interviewed and claimed that I had planted prescription drugs in her safe. I could not believe my ears!

I had absolutely no need to plant drugs . . . this woman was doctor-shopping like mad; she had thirty-five different prescriptions for her truly alarming pill habit. I'd seen her on more than one occasion literally falling down stairs, unable to even stand up straight. I was very indignant and called my attorney immediately, asking about what I could do to clear my name. He said, "You're not going to do a thing . . . this is the best PR you could ever get!" He was right . . . I let it go.

Marketing is simply the art of putting products or services in front of the people actively looking to buy them. If you're skeptical about marketing people, know that I am too. Marketing people tend to be obsessed with pretty graphs and nebulous stats like the number of likes a post gets on Facebook. I take a more pragmatic approach: I concentrate on doing the things that actually produce income for my clients.

So far, this philosophy has worked out pretty well for everyone: When the work my media company does doubles a client's income in the first year, my clients tend to pay the marketing bill before they pay the electric bill. My approach and results even won over a very hard-nosed businessman who has seen and heard every pitch in the world and tends to be quite skeptical: Tom Martin, of Martin Investigative Services. Here are some highlights of what I have shared with him over the years—advice that I know will work for you as well.

First and foremost, understand that your website is the single most important thing you can do with your marketing dollar. Think about it. All your marketing efforts (business cards, advertisements, e-mail signatures, and so on) point to your website. More importantly, from the standpoint of your potential customer, your website simply *is* your business.

Given the importance of your website, you may be thinking I'm going to say something like you need to make your website look professional. Or maybe, you have to make it show up in search engines. These things are absolutely important, and my firm spends a lot of time on these things for each and every client website.

However, these things are not enough. You might have the best-looking site in the world with tons of people looking at it every day. Still, your site won't actually produce inquiries or income unless you sell the potential customer on your goods and services and ask for their business. Accordingly, there are two astoundingly simple things you can do if you really want your website to make you more money. Let's talk about both of these things.

1. Speak to the Customer

Have you ever been at a party, in conversation with someone who talked about himself the whole time? This guy didn't listen to you. In fact, he didn't let you talk at all. All of his sentences began with "I" or "My." Guess what? This is how 99 percent of business websites in the world read: They are boring and self-centered.

In your daily web-browsing experience, how many sites do you come across with statements like, "We were voted the best in town" or "Our company has been the industry leader in [whatever] since 1988"? The potential customer doesn't care about you or how great you think your company is. What the potential customer cares about is what you can do for them.

Reexamine every part of your website with these goggles on. Does the content directly address the potential customer? It should:

- Outline what you can do for them
- Outline the benefits to them
- Outline your qualifications (as relevant to their needs)

- Speak in plain and simple language—at a level that even a sixth grader can understand

You'd think these things would be easy for a business owner to define. This is never the case. It's hard for anybody involved in running the day-to-day operations of a business to think about their industry from the perspective of the customer. It's usually easier and more cost-efficient just to hire my firm.

But I digress. There's a final bullet point you should consider putting into the list above:

- Set up a solution to the potential customer's problem

Let me illustrate this with an example from Martin Investigative Services. While Tom Martin has dozens of private investigators working for him, more often than not he answers the calls to his office personally. These inquiries usually come from potential customers looking to take advantage of martinpi.com's offer for a free consultation. Over the years, I have witnessed Tom handle dozens of these initial calls. Let me tell you how each and every one goes.

Tom asks each caller to clearly explain their specific situation and specific investigative need. Then he asks:

Do you want [this solution to your problem]?

This question is rhetorical; of course, they want a solution to their problem. Then Tom outlines the three basic things you need to know for any sale:

- The specific plan
- How long it's going to take
- How much it's going to cost

Sounds simple, right? Yet most businesspeople, let alone salespeople, don't bother to explain these three basic things to potential clients.

You can tie Tom's solution-based sales calls back into your marketing. You should likely put all of these solution-based elements on your website: What is the plan? How long is it going to take? How much is it going to cost? More or less, this is the same script your salespeople should be using too.

If you spend the time to make sure all the pages of your website speak directly to the potential customer, you're halfway to making your business a lot more money. What's the second half?

2. Ask the Customer for Their Business Often and in the Right Way

Have you ever been to a website where you had to dig through multiple pages just to find a simple phone number? How many of those times did you get fed up and try a different website instead? Chances are you were 100 percent ready to do business with the first company, but since they didn't bother making it easy for you to do so, they lost the sale.

In my experience, most people really only visit one page of a website. So if that one page (which is really every page of your website) doesn't make it easy to do business with you—forget it. People won't. So give them this information often. Here are three ways to do it.

First, the top of your website should have your phone number on it, at all times, regardless of what page you are on. This is relatively simple, but it gets better: Look up martinpi.com on a mobile phone. Note the big graphical "call" button that is there at all times? Click that and it actually functions to call Martin Investigative Services.

Second, ask for the sale multiple times within your content. The homepage of martinpi.com asks the potential customer to call or e-mail no less than seven times. This is known as a call to action, a push for the potential customer to become a lead or sale. On martinpi.com, we want potential customers to call or e-mail.

Finally, make it beneficial for the potential customer to call. As I mentioned earlier, http://www.martinpi.com offers a free, confidential consultation. To the potential customer who has a very real and pressing problem in their personal or professional life, this is a very tempting offer. Why not? It's free, I might as well call . . .

If you're serious about making money with your business, this means making your website revolve around the customer. Forget talking about yourself so much, and start talking about how you can help your potential customer. Ask for their business often and give them an incentive to call. It's worked for Martin Investigative Services, and it can work for your business.

Brian Chernicky

Owner, ImagineDynamic.com

2

MARITAL MISADVENTURES

I stopped at my neighborhood Pavilions grocery store last night on the way home from work to grab a few last-minute items for dinner. I was deciding which cheese to bring home when all of a sudden another cart crashed into mine and a female voice squealed, "I love you!" This is not a frequent occurrence in my life. I looked up, and there stood a classic real housewife of Orange County—blonde, slender, tan, wearing a tight designer dress that showed off a twelve-thousand-dollar boob job. She rushed over, gave me a big hug and kiss, and said, "You changed my life!"

This particular housewife had found herself embroiled in a messy divorce and was getting absolutely hammered in every way. She lost custody of her kids, she wasn't getting any support money, her bank accounts were frozen. You name it, everything was going wrong. Let me point out that we both live in Orange County, California, where it's very difficult for a mother to lose custody of her children. Something has got to be very wrong for that to happen, and there was nothing in her life to warrant such an action. This woman was simply not being adequately represented.

Her best friend was a client of mine, who brought her in to see me and asked if there was anything I might do to help at this point. It was a simple matter for me to choose what I thought would be the right fit for her from our "Best Of" attorney list and send them on their way. I had forgotten this encounter three weeks later, when she crashed her cart into mine. She announced triumphantly, "I'm getting alimony, I'm getting child support, my funds are unfrozen, and I've got the kids back at my house! *Thank you!*" She sashayed away with most eyes in the store on her.

The best part was the cashier standing behind the counter, who had watched this whole encounter bug-eyed. He leaned over after the housewife had moved on and asked in a hushed, incredulous voice, "You *know* her?"

"Yep," I said, and left it at that. I walked out to the parking lot, carrying my bag to my car with the California personalized MARTNPI plates and feeling quite pleased with myself. That was a nice end to the day. Every now and then I'm driving through town when someone spots that plate, and I get a big smile and thumbs-up. Sometimes, of course, I get a much ruder gesture from a different finger. That's a man, usually a disgruntled ex-spouse, pissed off because we caught him on a marital surveillance. The way I feel about that is simple: don't blame me because you were caught banging Mary Lou in your SUV in the school parking lot after the soccer game. That was all you, buddy.

Just another day in the life of a PI.

❊ ❊ ❊

Many PIs fancy themselves as real hard guys. They tend to come from military and law enforcement backgrounds, as I did, and pride themselves on toughness. They have an image of the PI in their minds: the dangerous guy in the trench coat. They are at a complete loss when faced with a crying, hysterical woman or worse, any discussion whatsoever of "feelings." They tend to alienate female clients with this attitude, which is shortsighted, as females make up 80 percent of my marital surveillance business.

It's hard to believe it's been more than thirty years since I took on my first official marital surveillance case. On that day I called my female client into my small office, where I dimmed the lights, pulled down a projection screen, and ran the film on an old-fashioned projector— that's how long ago this was. Together we watched the footage I'd shot of her husband groping and making out with their next-door neighbor. The second I turned the lights back on, I could see my client was taking this hard. She had literally turned green. Before I could say a word, she threw up all over my office.

In the hundreds of similar meetings I've had since that day, the same thing has happened at least fifteen times. The sight of a spouse being intimate with another causes some women to become immediately and violently ill, even though it's not the most unexpected news—they have a PI on the case, after all. Still, suspecting is one thing, seeing the truth with your own eyes is another. I now stock my office with barf bags and keep them at the ready for moments like this.

I felt terrible for my first marital client. I wanted to help her at what was certainly one of the most devastating moments of her life. I said what I could to comfort her, which at that moment wasn't much; I just didn't have the experience or resources to do more. A couple of years passed, the agency grew, and I handled more and more marital cases. What do you do, heading to work on a beautiful sunny Monday morning, knowing you've got five women on the schedule whose days are about to be ruined with surveillance footage of their hubbies from the previous weekend?

Most PIs I knew played the tape, handed it over, shook hands, and said good-bye and good luck. Finding the evidence is the job, after all, and it was done. I kept the bigger picture in mind. For every client thereafter, I developed a game plan, mostly involving referrals and follow-up. Today, I've got it down to a science. A woman comes to me because she thinks her husband is cheating, and we establish that he is indeed having an affair. At that point one-third of these women want to file for divorce immediately, one-third want to go to counseling, and the last third have no idea what the hell to do. We offer plenty of options. I usually don't charge for subsequent meetings, where we come up with an action plan and I make the crucial introductions they need. My clients pay a good fee for surveillance work. I'm not going to leave them high and dry at this vulnerable point.

It all depends on what's the next step they want to take. Marriage counselor? Private therapist? I've got numbers for the most skilled and empathetic relationship counselors all over Southern California. Unfortunately, marriage counseling is only an option when the husband is willing to go. Sometimes we never see the woman again after we hand over the evidence, because she's at a stalemate. She wants to go to counseling, he refuses, but she's not ready to leave the marriage. There's nothing more I can do for her.

For all the other women I say, "Okay, here's what you need to do. Get a good lawyer. That's the #1 most important thing. You must ensure you get the money you deserve coming to you. Alimony and child support—let's make sure your kids are taken care of all the way through college. That's priority number one."

I tell my clients the truth—gently—but they need to understand: you think watching this tape starring your husband is bleak? This is the *best* it's going to be for a good long while. Once you file divorce papers, things get truly ugly. That's why it is imperative that you have the right lawyer. The good news is that we're with our clients every step of the way. There does eventually come a day when things start to look up and life starts to turn around for the better.

The after-care plan for our clients includes investment advice, counseling referrals, even dating rules. Believe me, at this point I know what I'm doing. I have done this work so many times . . . it's clear to me after a fairly brief discussion of the situation just what will happen to these women and their kids. I've been invited to quite a few second weddings. These days I have clients from the nineties coming back to use me for their second divorce, or sending me their adult kids who are getting divorced.

I kept an ever-evolving list of sixteen or so family law attorneys we referred to in Orange County. Evolving because over the years attorneys would retire, some great ones would enter the field or come to town, others would move. . . . Still, there was a core list for many, many years of names that I consider the top of the top. I called it (unofficially) "The Top Ten" list and published it on my website as a public service. Over time, my list became known as "the" place for an attorney to land. You couldn't ask me to be on it, or pay me to be on it. Trust me, people tried. This was simply me providing not only my own clients but anybody who might need one with some good solid referrals.

We still keep the list, but eventually we had to take it off the site. Here in Orange County, with hundreds of millions of dollars at stake in many divorces, people started consulting the list and making appointments with the top five or six attorneys in town to prevent their spouse from being able to hire them in the event they divorced. All you have to do is show up for a consultation with an attorney—you don't have to retain them—but that consult will prevent your spouse from being able to use that attorney. It's just another tactic in high-stakes divorce, but it happened so frequently that eventually I felt I could no longer post the list publicly.

The next issue then became that people started dropping by our office for a consultation just to schmooze, hoping to get a copy of that list. We quickly arrived at the point where we now have to limit our free advice to one name per visit. What began as a good deed for those considering divorce could no longer be a free public service, but it did give Martin Investigative Services an unforeseen niche business.

MARTIN INVESTIGATIVE SERVICES
"Best Of"

As life and business hummed along over the years, my "top ten" list was becoming well-known in legal circles. Meanwhile, people looked to me for advice on everything. Neighbors would watch to see what gardeners we used at our house, for example, and try to hire them too. They (wisely) assumed that I would be using the best. A top-notch private investigator is highly skilled in interview, interrogation, and finding information. As a busy professional, why not find one in your area and take advantage of his skills?

I'm the most expensive PI in the country, and that's because I pay my employees the most. They deserve it, because they're the best of the best. But I will do research for you for a few hundred dollars. That fee is well within the average consumer's grasp! Especially when we are talking about major investments. Putting your retirement funds into a certain account is one example. Having a facelift is another. This is your hard-earned money we are talking about. Your face. Your life. Why would you not do some due diligence?

A good friend of mine was having cutting-edge heart surgery and said, "I'm thinking about using these two guys. They're brothers, supposed to be the best." A couple of my guys and I went down to the prestigious hospital where these surgeons practiced and started talking to the nurses. We learned, basically, that these two were the butchers of Baghdad in the heart field. But my friend was always the smartest guy in the room. Smarter than 90 percent because he had me investigate, just not smart enough to *take* my advice. They mangled his body, taking veins from his legs to transplant to his heart. He was in the hospital for two months recovering. A year later, sitting at his desk, he had a massive heart attack and died.

A man came to me to one day and said, "I'm having a lot of trouble with my teeth. I might need to replace them all. Who's the best dentist in the area?" In an image-conscious area like Southern California, there are thousands and thousands of cosmetic dentists. I personally know a good dentist, of course . . . mine. You think I don't do my research? When I moved to Newport Coast, I consulted the number-one dentist in Southern California who testifies against other dentists in malpractice trials and asked, "Who would you go to in these cases: a root canal, cosmetic dentistry, a general dentist?" He gave me a list, which I refer to on top of other research.

How about buying a car? I've bought or leased at least 200 Mercedes in my life. Not for me, for clients. Because if you know how to negotiate a car purchase and get the absolute best deal . . . and you take all your business there . . . it works out great. Find an investigator who knows the difference between leasing and buying and get him/her to help. Again, let me stress, this is not just a service for rich people. I can't even estimate the number of Hondas I've bought for clients. Then again, it can certainly be a service for rich people. . . . I've bought a couple planes! A yacht for $172 million! What did I know about yachts? Not much. What do I know about investigating and interviewing? Plenty. Now I also know quite a bit about yachts. Our client is enjoying his on the waters off the south of France.

Other things a PI can advise you on: Plastic surgeons. Cancer specialists. Attorneys. Whatever it is, there's a way to find out who is the best. The best gynecologist, landscaper, car mechanic. Best place to buy an engagement ring. Build your website. Book a cruise. Best travel agent? I've got the best one of a dying breed. Too many people just do it online themselves these days. You're investing thousands of dollars and your precious free time into your vacation. Why not make sure it goes right?

I hope you are getting the point that the list is endless. The idea of BEST OF lists led me to come up with a niche nobody else was doing. With solid interview and interrogation skills, we know how to retrieve information and get the job done. We will figure it out! Now, as far as you finding someone to do this for you, that goes for PIs as well. Go to a private eye who is licensed, in good professional standing, and has an office. Having an office doesn't make him a good investigator, necessarily, but it sure makes meetings easier and more professional. If he can afford an office, he should be doing all right.

Or call my office . . . we know the best investigators all over the country. I'll refer you. Not for money, not for a referral fee—I am way past all that. I want to see people take advantage of a resource that is sadly overlooked: the services of a first-class PI to make whatever major life decision you are facing easier!

* * *

At this point in my life and career it's funny to recall how naïve I once was. I seriously considered becoming a priest as a young man and spent four years in the seminary. Less than three months after graduation, I turned in my Bible, rosary beads, and robes for a badge, credentials, and a gun. I soon found myself on the seedy streets of Las Vegas, kicking in the door to a cheap motel room. A drug dealer was inside with a prostitute. We yanked him out of bed, cuffed him, and my partner Bill asked him, "How much did you pay for this girl?"

"A thousand dollars," the guy responded.

"For how long?"

"A couple hours," he said. This truly shocked me.

I pulled the girl aside. "Can I ask you something personal, just between you and me?" I was all of twenty-three years old and less than six months out of seminary school. "What the hell do you do, exactly, that's so special, to earn a thousand dollars?" My mind could not conceive of such a thing. The girl gave me a look. "You'll certainly never know," she huffed. Then she told my supervisor that I was prying into her personal life about what sex acts she performed. I got into a little hot water over that one. Meanwhile Bill was laughing his ass off.

A couple of weeks later we were in the Watts area of Los Angeles, kicking another door down, where inside we found a strung-out, skeletal woman doing her best to flush literally pounds of cocaine down the toilet. She wasn't doing a very good job; her coordination was gone. Her eyes were glassy and there was powder all over her face. . . . she was completely strung out. Wearing a torn negligee, she was the skinniest, dirtiest, most unattractive woman I'd seen in quite a while.

"If you don't mind me asking?" Bill said politely. "What did you do before you became a dope dealer?"

"I was on the street. A prostitute," she said sullenly.

"I can see why you got into this line of work then," Bill blurted. Another complaint. The "suits"—I would later become one myself— were not amused by this remark, and Bill got a three-day vacation from work.

❊ ❊ ❊

Many things have changed over time . . . the basic nature of men has not. Remember the three options with infidelity: divorce, counseling, or "I don't know what to do"? Things are quite different when it's a male client in my office. I have yet to have one man watch a video of his wife coming out of a hotel room with another guy and say, "You know, I think I'm going to try to work it out." Trust me. It just doesn't happen. Ninety-nine percent of the time the husband is out the door.

A middle-aged man who owned a software business and lived in the suburbs came in to see me once and said, "I think my wife is fooling around. But she's not leaving the house. I think someone is coming over to visit her."

We set up surveillance and on the third day a garbage truck pulled up, a guy jumped out of the passenger side, dumped the garbage cans, took a quick look around, and entered the house. He came back outside twenty minutes later adjusting his belt buckle and jumped back inside the truck. They got out of there in a hurry.

I called the client and said, "I've got some news for you. We did our job and found out who the guy is . . . please come in for the full report." He showed up at our office for the viewing of the video. I was pretty sure seeing this footage would absolutely devastate him; it's never a fun moment for anyone. He jumped out of his seat at the point the guy emerged from his own front door.

"I can't believe it! I cannot believe what I am seeing!" he shouted.

"I know it's quite a shock. We will work this out. We are going to find you a good attorney . . . " I began.

He was absolutely raging. "I can't believe that bitch would do this to me!"

"It's very hard when these things happen in life . . . sometimes the people we trust . . . "

"No, you don't understand . . . my wife is a complete ignorant dumbass *bitch*!"

"Believe me, I do understand much better than most how you feel . . . it's a terrible feeling of betrayal when a spouse fools around . . . "

"No! I'm pissed because she's doing the *garbage* guy! And she couldn't even get the *driver*. . . . she's banging the loser who dumps the cans?"

I thought I'd heard it all but this was a new one. "So you'd feel better if it had been the driver having an affair with your wife?"

"Yeah, that would be one hell of a lot better than this!"

It was a good reminder of something I've learned about all too well in this business—never underestimate a man's ego.

* * *

That saying about "What happens in Vegas, stays in Vegas" is very true. Las Vegas is the most dangerous city in America for a marriage. Something strange takes over when men head there. We've coordinated with local licensed investigators in Nevada and done plenty of surveillances on men heading on a "business trip" to Vegas. They tend to kiss the wife, leave their house, get in the car, drive to the airport, and park . . . the whole time being very careful should anyone happen to be observing. But something takes over once they pass through security and get to their gate. All hell breaks loose.

They meet their girlfriends in the waiting area to board the flight and start making out right then and there. . . . it's like they're in college again, never-never land. Same thing on the return. . . . they give their date a passionate good-bye kiss as they part. They go down to baggage claim, collect their bags, and revert back to loving husband and father, as if nothing ever happened. Some men wait until they arrive to find someone . . . or meet a "professional." Super Bowl, when thousands of men head to Vegas, is one of our busiest days all year. It's like shooting fish in a barrel.

Still, every now and then there's a curveball. I had a big one when I was just starting out. The man who walked into my office was straight out of *GQ*: a good-looking young Caucasian man, perfect haircut, beautiful suit. "I want you to do an investigation for me."

"What can I help you with?" I asked.

He handed over a videotape . . . an old-fashioned VHS tape. "Please take this tape and watch it. It's my wife having a baby."

"Excuse me?" I said. "I don't really want to watch your wife giving birth. . . . I'm not sure it's appropriate."

"Oh, it's appropriate all right," the man said. "When you finish watching, I will pay you a five-thousand-dollar retainer to represent me." This was at a time I was charging about a hundred dollars per case. I couldn't afford to turn down this business.

I didn't even have a tape player in the office, so I took the tape home that night and watched it. As promised, it was a hospital room scene with a beautiful young blond woman in the hospital giving birth. My potential client had shot this home movie. When the baby came out and the doctor held him up, the infant was black. There was a stunned silence in the delivery room, then the tape recorder crashed to the ground and the screen went dark. The tape was over. My client had fainted dead away.

I called him in the next day. "So . . . you're clearly not the father." I undertook an investigation and tracked down the guy. We learned that "Black Caesar" had been an entertainer at a bachelorette party that had taken place in Las Vegas a few nights before their wedding. There had been quite a lot of drinking going on . . . the night was very hazy . . . the wife could barely remember what had happened. Quite a lot had apparently happened. Bride and groom both assumed she got pregnant on the honeymoon a week later . . . both were beyond shock in the delivery room.

"There's really nothing more to find out," I told him. That was a quick marriage . . . over and officially done less than a year after their elaborate wedding. At the time it certainly got my attention . . . now I have a million stories like that. My point is that while it's usually men acting up in Vegas, it's an equal opportunity playground. Everyone needs to keep a lid on it!

❀ ❀ ❀

It's now easier than ever to "catch" a cheating partner on your own. We never recommend that someone do their own surveillance. There are several compelling reasons why this is not a good idea. The best is because very few men and women are prepared for what comes next, which could literally be anything from a parking lot brawl to a heart attack to murder. As a veteran of thousands of marital surveillances, I've seen all that and more.

Let a professional do the job. Don't bring yourself down to the level of an unfaithful spouse; stay above the fray. I would never, under any circumstances, allow a client to accompany me on surveillance, like they do on reality shows such as *Cheaters*, for example. That's my best advice, but for whatever reason, let's say you choose to ignore it. Let's say you just don't have the money to hire a PI and want to know what to do.

I would tell you that it's generally pretty easy: give your spouse enough rope to hang him- or herself. By that I mean that people engaged in an affair are always eager to see their partner in crime. They are constantly looking for reasons to get away from the house. Give them plenty of room. Tell him or her that you are going out for the evening, or better yet, away to Mom's for the weekend. Make sure they see you pulling out of the driveway all dressed up, or carrying a suitcase, or whatever your excuse is.

Chances are excellent that after an hour, to make sure you won't double back because you forgot something, your partner will be racing out the door for a little hanky-panky. Sadly, it usually doesn't take much time or effort to catch a cheater. The vast majority of our marital surveillances last for four to eight hours—or less!

❀ ❀ ❀

If there is one question I am asked more than any other, it's what the most common signs of a cheating spouse are. The list below applies to both men and women, but for simplicity's sake I have referred to the cheating spouse as "him." Also, a solid 80 percent of my clients are women, so it's generally men we are surveilling. Women are probably more intuitive and tuned in when it comes to thinking something is up, but men are also far less likely to suspect that their wife would ever dream of cheating on them.

TOP TWENTY SIGNS YOUR PARTNER IS CHEATING

1. "I'm Going to the Gym"

Your spouse spends more time than usual looking at himself in the mirror and has a newfound commitment to improving his physique. He starts a strict workout regimen that takes up a great deal of his free time. Or he might join a new gym and make a big show of leaving with his bag every day, but his appearance never changes. In either case, even as he raves about his new routine, he doesn't want you to work out at the same gym.

2. Extra Grooming

Along with shaping up, a sudden interest in diets, new clothing, haircuts, and more-frequent-than-usual showers are also telltale signs. Sure, he may just be boosting his self-esteem, but there's another common reason for this "extra effort." I usually put it this way: Ladies, if your husband starts coming home from a long day of work smelling better than when he left, you've got a problem.

3. A Change in Habits

Your husband has come home from work every day for the past ten years at 5 p.m. on the dot, but recently he's been coming home at 8 or 9 p.m., pleading more work at the office. You used to beg him to walk the dog at night, now they're gone for an hour every night without needing to be asked. Out of the blue he takes up a hobby like hiking or fishing that takes him out of the house for long periods of time.

4. Your Company Is No Longer Desired

Your spouse discourages you from joining him for happy hours with his friends or activities you frequently joined him on, such as camping. There are some valid reasons why you can't always come along, but he should be making an attempt to involve you.

5. Glued to the Phone

Your partner is engaging in an unusually high amount of text messaging and e-mailing. He starts to keep his phone close to him at all times. He receives texts from unfamiliar numbers or with codes like "11691." He starts locking the phone or changes the security password.

6. Locked in the Office

Every night your spouse locks himself away behind closed doors with the computer, claiming he needs to work or catch up on news. Meanwhile, the browser is reset to "private" and he's suddenly started wiping the search engine history clean every day.

7. Business Trips

Suddenly your partner starts traveling for business, even though his job duties haven't changed. Or business trips that used to be brief now start on Friday and require an entire weekend of preparation for a Monday presentation. He says it's against company policy to bring you along.

8. Excessive Overtime

His duties and paychecks are the same but his workload seems to have doubled. He now works late into the night and weekends. And why won't he discuss the details of that huge, time-consuming project he's now on? He refuses to meet near his office for a late-night date, explaining that he can't be interrupted.

9. Absences

He finds reasons not to participate in family events, saying he needs to help a friend move or catch up on a work project while the house is quiet. He finds every excuse to avoid big family gatherings but insists that you go ahead without him.

10. Checked Out

Even when he's physically present, he's not all there. He stops asking about your day or inquiring about your friends. He no longer seems interested in stories about your boss or mother. You can't seem to pin him down to plan vacations and holidays. His mind seems to be elsewhere much of the time.

11. Unexplained Expenditures

He earns the same amount of money as usual but less of it seems to come home. He makes excessive ATM withdrawals, but he can't point to any large purchases to explain where the money went. He's suddenly always short of cash, borrowing from you when you're out together. One obvious explanation: Affairs are costly. There are dinners, gifts, and getaways to pay for!

12. Secretive Accounts

You used to have an open-door policy concerning shared finances, but now he insists on handling it all. He accuses you of snooping in his wallet or briefcase, or maybe even hides them. Balancing the checkbook and the credit card bills are now loaded topics due to his secretive and defensive attitude.

13. Social Media

Your spouse is spending far too much time corresponding with and following a certain person (or new group). Never underestimate how foolish cheaters can be: plenty of people get caught because they actually post photos of themselves in the company of their significant others to their accounts, or mention when and where they're going for a dinner or getaway, or one of their "friends" posts an indiscreet update about them.

14. Buying Jewelry

He's taken to wearing gold rings or chains for the first time. Or you find out that he's buying women's jewelry but you haven't seen any of it. Could it be a transgender fantasy? Nah.

15. Unexplained Items

He keeps cologne, hairspray, or blankets in his car. Random ticket stubs, hotel keys, greeting cards, lipstick holders, earrings, and condom wrappers find their way into your home without explanation.

16. Hang-Ups

The number of hang-up telephone calls at your home landline has jumped. But when he answers the phone, someone's always on the other end. You see him on a different mobile phone than he normally uses, or find an extra disposable one in his car's glovebox.

17. Less Sex

He used to always be ready for sex, despite mood, workload, or stress level. Lately, you've expressed interest and he's hesitant. When he comes to bed, it's straight to sleep with no pillow talk.

18. Evasiveness, Defensiveness, and Prickliness

He no longer freely offers information. He starts an argument when you ask about his plans, thereby avoiding the question and making you think twice before you quiz him again. He gets on your case when you ask something simple, like how his day was. He's irritable and easily provoked. Fights are more frequent, and they never get resolved.

19. No More Surprises

He is not pleased when you drop by his office unannounced, even if you've been doing it for years. Maybe there's a good reason he doesn't want you to meet any of the new female employees. Or he doesn't want you to realize that he's out on a three-hour "business lunch" or to hear any office gossip.

20. Obvious Lies

Your partner claims he's been spending time with a buddy when you accidentally run into the buddy's wife, who innocently asks why it's been so long since they've seen him. Or two of your girlfriends saw your live-in boyfriend with a woman at a bar, but when you question him about it, he swears he was working late. When it's come to the point that your partner is blatantly and carelessly lying, it is most definitely time to take a serious look at what's going on.

As a family law attorney who has been practicing for nearly four decades, I'd like to share what I see as some of the biggest mistakes people make when they divorce. Hopefully, I can steer readers away from costly and painful missteps.

Men and women don't handle divorce differently. There is one major variable that matters: who has the earning ability and therefore confidence versus who is financially dependent and frightened because their entire livelihood is currently at risk. I have represented many powerful women who are paying substantial support to men. However, I represent far more men who pay spousal support to their former wives.

First and foremost, if you are getting divorced, you must find the right lawyer. Don't just pick a lawyer because you skimmed his or her site on the Internet. Sure, you can use it as a resource, but don't believe half of what you see or read on the Internet (that goes for more than just choosing an attorney). Go with word of mouth from trusted sources like friends and family members, and obviously check experience and credentials.

Observe at your first meeting the kind of office where he or she works. If it's somebody with an Ikea desk in a shared office making copies at Kinko's, think twice. You want a successful lawyer. An attorney who is scrambling to make the mortgage payment every month will be on to the next thing as soon as he or she gets your retainer. Look for an attorney with a reputable, substantial practice and adequate, well-trained staff so that you will never be left high and dry. Divorce is a crisis practice; you need someone available to you almost 24/7.

Pay close attention to the words he or she uses. If he or she says things like, "It always goes that way" or "that will never happen," get up and leave. There are no absolutes in the law. Same goes for somebody who tells you that they never lose a case. All I can say to that is they have not been practicing law very long.

Truly, the most important factor is whether or not you and the attorney "click." Your attorney will be in a close fiduciary relationship with you; it's important that you get along, understand them, and can communicate clearly with them. They will be helping you with decisions that will affect the rest of your life.

Next, in no particular order:

- Payback. I often see men and women use divorce as a forum for acrimony. It's the platform used to point out all of the other person's inadequacies and wrongdoings. They are thinking: I am going to repay every single hurt you have inflicted on me. I will teach you a lesson. If you're going to try to hurt somebody else, you will probably wind up hurting yourself. These things have a way of boomeranging. I truly believe that when you leave this earth all that matters is how you affected others. Revenge is overrated.
- Expecting things to be different. I am amazed that people expect their former spouse to change during or after the divorce, despite the fact that they absolutely refused to change throughout the entire duration of the marriage. If he or she was an inattentive parent while you were married, he or she will not morph into a doting parent now that you're divorcing. If he or she was casual about money, he or she is not going to suddenly become financially responsible and frugal. In fact, these traits will only become magnified during the stress of a divorce. People simply can't understand why the divorce process does not force the other person to do what they "should" do. Please believe me, that is not its purpose.
- Manage expectations. Most people spend very little time before consulting with their attorney for the first time about what it is they really want out of the divorce. Other than, "I want to get him or her!" of course. I ask my client at our first meeting, "What's your goal?" and then try to match it with my job requirements. Let's say somebody has custody and business issues; my job is to maximize your time with your child and minimize your financial exposure.

   Years ago a gentleman came in to consult me. He was divorcing his spouse of decades; they had five kids together. He sat down and said, "She's getting nothing." I said, "I am not the lawyer for you, because that's not going to happen." I also had a woman come in to see me. She had been married six weeks—honestly, not a day longer. She told me, "I want lifetime support; I deserve it. I gave him the best days of my life." That must have been one hell of a six weeks, I thought, but still, she was another client I had to decline to represent.

- Compromise. We have a saying in divorce: If both people walk out of a settlement unhappy, then we probably had a great settlement. If one walks out thinking, "I really screwed the other side!" then there are guaranteed to be problems later on. Settlement means compromise; it does not mean "I get everything I want." The trick for a good lawyer is to make sure the compromises tilt in his or her client's favor.
- Taking things personally. Remember this: marriage is personal; divorce is business. Marriage is one of the closest, most binding intimate relationships a person will ever have. Divorce is a legal process.
- Expecting fairness. I don't ever use the word fair when it comes to the divorce process. I tell my clients "fair" is a four-letter word beginning with the letter F. What is fair for you is definitely not what the other side will consider fair for them. I encourage my clients to substitute "reasonable" for fair. So many clients rage and despair. . . . "This isn't fair . . . he (or she) gets this . . . he (or she) got that. It's just not fair!" Maybe it is; maybe it's not, but it's probably reasonable. That is what matters here.
- Refusing responsibility. Many clients want to abdicate responsibility for their own actions during the divorce, as they probably did throughout the marriage as well. My divorce clients are my partners. I require that they participate in this process. I don't make decisions for them; I will guide them and lay down parameters, but ultimately they must make decisions and live with the consequences. It is their life and their divorce. When a client tells me, "I don't understand accounting," I say, "Well, you're going to learn. The left column and the right column need to line up . . . that's pretty much it!"

A "good divorce" can be had, if both parties are willing to do the work. Certainly, divorce can and does tear families apart. However, I have seen many divorces where former marital partners become friends and cooperative co-parents. This can happen for you, if you will do what it takes to make it so. Here's a big incentive: your children will come out of a "good" divorce far more intact than they will from an ugly, mud-slinging divorce.

The most exciting thing about representing my clients is watching someone who has never been empowered, for whatever reason, become self-sufficient. Divorce can be a chance for a woman to stand on her own two feet for maybe the first time in her life. She can make her own choices and eventually become the very best person she is capable of being. My clients often undergo this process, because I won't have it any other way! I will do whatever it takes to help them become self-sufficient, whether that means getting them to downsize, learn how to handle finances, explore career opportunities, go back to school . . . whatever it takes. No one wants to go through another divorce, so make sure you can live and thrive on your own, not just move on to the next partner and repeat all the same mistakes.

Here's a final word of advice for you: stay married if you can! How does one do that? Well, I like to say to my friends and family members that staying married can be as simple as making a choice. Not easy, but simple. (Note: I am not talking about situations where there is abuse, violence, or any other compelling reason to leave and not look back.) Life is a series of choices every day, but there's one major choice you can make when it comes to your marriage: you can be right, or you can be happy. I personally have been married for forty years. Can you guess which one I chose?

Lisa Hughes, CPA, CFLS
Hughes and Hughes
Tustin, California

3

THE NUTS AND BOLTS OF DIVORCE

Any PI worth his salt has been through hundreds of divorce cases. Hopefully, my clients will only have to endure one in their lifetime. As discussed, my goal is for my clients to be as well-prepared as possible for everything that's coming up. I start with my own work product: our surveillance is summarized in a complete written report accompanied by photos and video.

California, where I do most of my business, is what is known as a no-fault state (though all fifty states now have some form of "no fault" divorce on the books). That means someone can have sex with ten men or women in the town square at high noon and it won't affect their divorce proceedings; in fact, these acts are not even admissible in court. So why do people turn to private investigators for proof of affairs when they are divorcing, and why do we go to such lengths to make sure it is impeccably documented? Simple. When it comes time to split, if you've had an affair, it gives the other side leverage.

You may wish to protect and keep the name of your paramour out of all proceedings. You may come from a religious or cultural background that frowns upon cheating, and the public shame will be devastating to you. You may wish to conceal you've had an affair from your parents or children. In certain professions, the admission you've had an affair can be highly detrimental to your business. It's worth sweetening the pot to keep that kind of stuff quiet. That's why people need proof of infidelity. These are also all good reasons not to have an affair in the first place.

I am not ashamed to say that after three decades of dealing with divorce-related matters the fact that adultery is still actually technically illegal in many places came as a big surprise to me. In the book *Adultery: Infidelity and the Law*, Stanford University law professor Deborah Rhode reminded me that as of the year 2016, twenty-one states still have criminal prohibitions on adultery. Something to keep in mind as you work on a troubled marriage, or navigate your own divorce!

A UNIQUE CASE OF DIVORCE

Many years ago a man showed up in my office and said, "I'd like you to follow my wife. I think she's cheating on me." Not an unusual request; we'd handled a thousand cases just like this. So I followed the wife one afternoon from her home as she headed to the school her kids attended. Picking them up from school, I assumed. But no.

A man emerged from a back door of the building, looked around furtively, and then got into the passenger side of her vehicle. I followed her suburban minivan as they headed to a local 24-hour gym and parked in a faraway corner of the underground garage. Soon enough, that van was rocking and rolling. Our client was outraged to discover that his wife was cheating on him with their daughter's third-grade teacher. The first words out of his mouth after he viewed the photos were, "I'm going to sue her."

"Well, we can definitely recommend a good family law attorney for you. Certainly you can file for divorce as the petitioner, but you can't sue her. You'll file, she'll respond, and eventually it will be dismissed. That's how it works," I explained.

"No, I'm going after her. For alienation of love and affection." I thought he was being a bit ridiculous and vengeful. I thought he should simply file for divorce and do his best to move on with his new life and custody arrangement. Instead, he went to court, sued both his wife and the teacher for alienation of affection, and won! As his private investigator of record, I testified in the divorce hearing. Unfortunately, the wife appealed the decision, the appellate court ruled in her favor, and it all faded away as one of those strange but true legal cases.

DON'T LET FINANCIAL IGNORANCE GET IN THE WAY

In recent years the term "financial infidelity" has gotten a lot of play in the media. "Financial infidelity" is simply committing any form of dishonesty about financial matters. This could range from lying to a spouse about how much a pair of shoes or golf clubs cost, squirreling cash away in a box for a rainy day, or establishing secret bank accounts in another state. There are numerous estimates that as many as half of all American couples engage in some type of this behavior. In the world of divorce and private investigation, this form of "cheating" is hardly a new or uncommon phenomenon.

I'd like to address something that is far more common and dangerous. That is financial ignorance within a marital relationship. This issue is prevalent in high-income areas like Orange County, where our corporate offices are located in the heart of Newport Beach. It is particularly prevalent among our female clients, who make up the vast majority of our "marital" cases. Though there are many cases of wealthy women who support spouses, in this day and age females still tend to be the financially dependent partner, as well as the one who cedes control of handling finances.

There are countless women in Southern California and the United States living in a bubble. A very pretty, shiny bubble, but a fragile bubble nonetheless. These women live in beautiful homes and drive expensive cars. They have a wallet full of credit cards and accounts at restaurants and clubs and never see a bill. They sign whatever tax forms or financial papers are put in front of them without reading them. They don't know how much their husbands make or spend and don't care, because life is great. Until the wheels come off.

I usually come in right about here, generally after a husband has been caught cheating and the wife has decided to file for divorce. Let's consider one hundred female clients I see here in a typical year at the office. They sit in front of me listening as I list different options: one, a basic asset search; two, bank, savings, and checking account searches; and three, stocks, bonds, and securities searches we may need to run. Three-quarters of these women look at me like I'm from the planet Mars. They don't have any idea what these terms mean. Even worse, they have zero knowledge of the financial affairs in their own household.

Things have generally been rocky for some time at home in these situations, so it's no secret to the man that the wheels were about to come off his marriage. By this time he's had some advance warning and been able to dissipate and/or hide many of the assets before any legal or investigative proceedings begin. It will now be much more difficult for us to locate these assets and get a true financial picture. If all women knew where their household bank accounts were located and had an accurate financial understanding of their joint affairs, they would be so far ahead of the game. Not just in times of trouble, but always.

My clients come from every income level, and this display of financial ignorance is equally common in what I call "pots and pans" divorces, where there are very few assets to divide and there's no wealth involved on either side. The wife gets the pots and the husband gets the pans. Across the board, I would estimate that seven out of ten women do not have a clue about the family finances. It doesn't matter if you have $10,000 worth of assets or $10 million. In households where assets are north of ten million, the percentage jumps to nine out of ten women.

How many times have I been faced with a woman who has decided to divorce her husband? Thousands, and the numbers don't lie. They sit in front of me, grieving and still shocked that what they thought was a fairy-tale marriage has fallen apart so spectacularly. Then my questions start: "How much does your husband make?" "How much is your house worth?" "How much did you pay in taxes last year?" "Where is your money held?" They look at me blankly, and soon enough they're not only sad, but panicked. Because they don't know the answers . . . not even one of them. Like I said: if this is an average-income woman? This is the reaction I get 75 percent of the time. If she's a very rich woman, 90 percent of the time. I've been doing this kind of work for a very long time, and I stand by these numbers.

Please, readers . . . ask yourself honestly if you can answer these questions right now. If you are in the roughly ten to twenty percent of informed, empowered women, good for you! If you're not, it's never too late to start. Remember, ignorance is never bliss, particularly the financial kind. If you don't know where the assets are, or they can't be located by your private investigator, you will be splitting or getting half of nothing should your marriage end. That's what far too many women end up with: nothing.

✿ ✿ ✿

All right, moving ahead with filing for divorce: Work product in hand, initial appointment scheduled with the best family law practitioner for my client's particular situation. To ensure that their meeting will be productive, I ask my clients to do some written "homework."

First: Come up with a brief timeline of the events concerning the marriage. Start with basic information on each spouse (DOB, education, current job). Then cover the major milestones in the relationship: date of marriage, children and dates of birth, date of separation, and reason for separation. Be sure to list any extenuating circumstances such as drug or alcohol abuse, domestic violence, cheating, and the like. This document will serve as an excellent introduction to the players and what's involved at the first attorney meeting.

Second: Make a simple list of assets and debts, to the best of their knowledge. Unfortunately, many of my clients do not have a clue. Gather all available materials, including most recent tax returns, checking and savings accounts information, and stocks, bonds, securities, and retirement and pension plans.

Finally: Tell your attorney the three worst things your spouse will say about you. Forewarned is forearmed. Outline why, if applicable, you should get primary custody of the child or children.

Questions always began to fly at me fast and furious as my clients began to consider the implications of a new life on their own. I took notes at these sessions, and eventually created a long list culled from meetings with hundreds of women, facing every sort of situation. Of course, every divorce is unique, and many questions won't apply to your specific situation. You will have your own individual concerns that others don't, such as how do we split a Ferrari, or a horse? However, this is a broad list that covers most marital situations.

Take out a yellow highlighter and review the entire list of 155 questions. Highlight those that relate to your situation and are most urgent to you. Run through the entire list, and at the end you should be able to compile a list of your top five or seven or just the one most pressing issue. Prepare your timeline and asset/debt ratio as described above, and you'll be ready to sit down with your attorney. Doing your homework will reassure him or her that you're serious about divorcing and ready to pull the trigger. I want my clients to be an active participant in the meeting, not just sitting there afraid, not knowing what's coming, waiting to be told what to do next. My goal is for them, and you, to be as empowered as possible!

QUESTIONS TO CONSIDER

1. What immediate action should I take if I am planning to separate?
2. Should I take some, all, or none of the money currently in the joint accounts?
3. Can I cancel my life insurance after I file for divorce?
4. Can I change the beneficiaries on my IRA, 401(k), life insurance, and the like after I file for divorce?
5. Can I draft a new will/trust after I file?
6. Can I terminate the joint tenancy deed to my properties after I file for divorce?
7. I put the down payment on a house with my separate property. Will I get that money back?
8. If I sell stock after the separation, what happens if it goes up? Is a large tax due?
9. I'm fifty-nine years old. Can I just quit work to avoid paying child support?
10. I had the business before we were married. Does my spouse have an interest in it now?
11. I don't want to pay my spouse for 50 percent of the value of my business. Can I just give my spouse the business or close it down? Can I close it down and then reopen it as a new entity across the street?
12. I'm planning on filing for divorce next month. Will it hurt me if I expand the business at this time?
13. Should I take my year-end bonus or just leave it in the company?
14. Am I entitled to a share of my spouse's bonus that was earned partially before separation and partially after separation?
15. Is my prenuptial valid?
16. I paid tax on my spouse's community property income from community funds. Should the community be reimbursed?

17. What determines the date of separation?
18. Is the separation date important?
19. Does it matter if we go to counseling / have sex / go out to dinner / exchange gifts after the separation?
20. What are the benefits of mediation?
21. Can one attorney represent both parties?
22. At what age can children decide with which parent to live?
23. I'm going to inherit money eventually; will it have an effect on any divorce settlement?
24. I had my retirement fund established before my marriage. Will my spouse be entitled to any portion of it?
25. Will my spouse receive part of my stock options?
26. Does it matter if options are partially vested?
27. What can I do if I think my spouse is hiding assets? How can I find them?
28. Will the court order the parties to pay for half of tuition for private school or college for the children?
29. How long until I am divorced? What steps are necessary to complete the case? Can we shorten or speed up the process in any way?
30. How much can I receive in support? How is it determined? How can I get an order for child/spousal support?
31. Will I have to testify in court?
32. Can I keep the house? How long will I be able to stay in the house? Can I force my spouse to sell the house now?
33. Can I continue to be a stay-at-home parent?
34. Can I get 50/50 custody? What is joint legal custody? What is joint physical custody? How can I get full custody?
35. Can I get my spouse to pay my divorce attorney fees?
36. What happens when you go to court?
37. Should I pay community debts while the divorce action is pending?
38. Should I make repairs/improvements to the house before separation?
39. Should I use community property credit cards?
40. Can I charge my attorney's fees on a community credit card?
41. Should I cancel all the joint credit cards?

42. Can I sell any property or community property assets (car, stocks, and so on)?
43. Can I buy new real property or refinance during dissolution?
44. How much will the divorce cost?
45. How much of a retainer is required? Is the divorce case a flat fee?
46. Should I move out? How will it hurt me if I leave?
47. Do people stay in the same house during the divorce?
48. What is the effect upon custody if I stay in the house with the children or leave? Will this be considered abandonment? What can I take with me if I leave?
49. Do mothers always get full custody?
50. How does the court determine custody?
51. Can either party move out of state with the children?
52. What is a standard/typical custody and visitation order?
53. What is "family support"?
54. How long does spousal support last?
55. How do you define separate property?
56. How are 401(k)s and IRAs divided?
57. How do you divide a pension?
58. How do you divide furniture?
59. Can I get reimbursed for pre-separation expenditures of my spouse?
60. Is fault an issue?
61. Can I date while separated? Will it affect the divorce?
62. Can I handle this divorce without an attorney?
63. How do you initiate a divorce/papers?
64. Is a person charged rent if he or she stays in the house after separation?
65. If I owned the house before marriage, does my spouse now own a portion of it?
66. How are debts divided?
67. What is the effect of a written agreement resolving divorce issues?
68. How do I get my spouse to move out?
69. Who pays attorneys' fees? Do I have to pay my spouse's attorney's fees? Does my spouse have to pay any part of my attorney's fees?

70. Who is responsible for the mortgage payment? Who pays for the house while I am there?
71. Can I move out with our children?
72. Am I responsible for my spouse's debts incurred during our marriage if the credit card is only in my spouse's name?
73. I am a supported spouse. Should I get a job?
74. Who pays the bills right now?
75. What should I do with my paycheck?
76. What should I do with the money in our joint accounts?
77. Should I open a new bank account?
78. How are the assets divided up? How do we put a value on them?
79. My spouse didn't pay much attention to the children during the marriage, so why should my spouse get much time with them now?
80. My name is on title to the property we share; do we own the asset equally?
81. Are the oral agreements my spouse and I made before and/or during marriage valid?
82. My retirement/pension is not accessible now. Can it still be divided?
83. My spouse had a number of credit cards that I just discovered, and my spouse made a number of charges I did not know about. Am I still liable?
84. If I pay against community credit cards, will I get credit somehow?
85. Are spousal support payments taxable?
86. Who pays the taxes/declares taxes?
87. Does the judge consider the fact that my expenses are greater than my income?
88. Can my spouse keep me away from our children? Can I keep my spouse away from our children?
89. Should we file a joint tax return?
90. Can I get an annulment?
91. What is the difference between separation, legal separation, and dissolution?
92. From who do you need declarations to support my point of view?
93. Can the other party change our children's school, doctor, child care, and the like without my consent?

94. How do I get the district attorney off my back?

95. If the DA suspends my license, how do I get it (professional license, driver's license) back?

96. What can I do to stop wage garnishment?

97. What kind of change is the court looking for in order to modify custody/visitation?

98. Is there anything I can do to plan/protect myself financially before commencing this divorce action? What can I do to protect myself financially after the divorce action is filed?

99. Can my spouse be removed from the residence?

100. We own our own business. How do I prove what the other party earns and what the business is worth?

101. What can the court do if I am caught trying to hide assets?

102. What can the court do if I fail to tell my spouse about a specific asset or significant facts about an asset?

103. Do we have to go to court or can we reach an agreement between ourselves? Are there any other alternatives?

104. How does the case start?

105. Does it matter which party files?

106. Is there any benefit to filing first or waiting to be served?

107. If I decide to file first, how does my spouse get served?

108. What is the best way to serve my spouse?

109. What should I do if my spouse gets mad when service is made?

110. Am I legally separated now?

111. How will I know when I am separated?

112. What kind of witnesses do I need to prove the kind of person my spouse is?

113. What has to be done before I can be divorced?

114. What is the legal process of divorce? What is discovery?

115. How do you make certain the spousal support is tax-deductible?

116. How long will the spousal support order be?

117. How long will the child support order be?

118. My spouse and I agreed to pay for our children's college educations; can that promise be enforced?

119. My spouse runs his/her own business and I know he/she is running a lot of expenses through the business. How will I know what his/her true income is?

120. I do not work now but I have in the past. What number will the court use for my income?

121. How can I enforce the support order(s) if my spouse does not pay?

122. Should I have my mail sent elsewhere?

123. What records do you need to see about our financial assets?

124. What if my spouse shows up at school and just takes the children?

125. What are my options at this point?

126. How do I get a child's preference on where to live into evidence or before a judge? Will that child have to testify?

127. What is a 730 evaluation?

128. What are the advantages and disadvantages of doing a 730 evaluation?

129. What is the cost of a 730 evaluation?

130. What if we are unable to reach an agreement about custody?

131. Can I live with a person of the opposite sex? Are there any disadvantages to doing so? If so, what are they?

132. Is it okay for me to negotiate directly with my spouse? Are there any specific things that I need to be careful about discussing?

133. How will you let my spouse know we are open to settlement?

134. What if there are extraordinary expenses for repairs or maintenance of the house? Whose responsibility is it to pay?

135. I put some inheritance money into our home. How do I recoup that?

136. Is there a difference as to whether I hire an appraiser, expert, private detective, and the like, as opposed to my attorney hiring that individual?

137. I signed the house over to my spouse because he/she said it would make it easier to get a loan. Do I still have any interest in that house?

138. How can I make sure my spouse doesn't get rid of clothing / furniture / personal effects?

139. How will my jewelry be divided?

140. Who determines what each one of us gets in terms of property?

141. We have some stock options and my spouse wants to exercise them; should I agree? Are there any tax traps involved with this exercise?

142. Who determines which car each of us gets?

143. What can I do to ensure my spouse does not hold up or delay the divorce process?

144. How can I get my spouse's business records if he/she will not cooperate?

145. How can I protect myself from my spouse's harassing calls and visits?

146. My spouse's parents are claiming they have an interest in our business/property, what can I do?

147. How do I make sure my spouse keeps up health insurance on my kids and me?

148. Can my spouse be ordered to maintain health insurance for me or the kids after the divorce is finalized?

149. Can I force my spouse to name me as beneficiary on his/her life insurance?

150. How does the court determine the attorney's fee issue?

151. My parents gifted us with family heirlooms. Can I claim these for myself?

152. What do I say at the custody mediation appointment?

153. How do I make sure my credit is not ruined if my spouse does not pay the credit card bills / debt?

154. How do I maintain my own good credit record?

155. How do you determine if a debt is community or separate?

Several clients of ours have been killed by their spouses over the years—unfortunately, not such an unusual occurrence in marital work. It is a very natural human tendency to want to punish someone who has hurt you. However, some people involved in extremely contentious divorces are out for blood.

I have had to caution a number of clients—men and women both—who want to keep sticking it to them, sticking it to them, sticking it to them some more . . . "All right," I interject at some point. "I need to caution you that we've had a number of clients who are no longer with us."

"What do you mean?"

"I mean that they are dead. Murdered. Killed by their former spouse."

Clients are always surprised to receive this warning. They've never even considered such a thing. Well, I'm here to tell you that you should think about it. Do what you need to do to protect your interests, then let the professionals handle as much as possible. Divorce is hard on all concerned, and everyone has a breaking point. Do not drive a former spouse into dangerous rage and despair by deliberately pushing their buttons over and over in a misguided attempt to make them pay.

It can be nearly unbearable to see someone who has behaved despicably appear to "win"—especially when it's your money, home, kids, pets, reputation, or all of the above on the line. Still, it's imperative to rein in feelings of vengeance as much as possible. Try to remember that this too shall pass, and one day you will be beyond this. Everyone loses many things in a divorce. Don't let your life be one of them.

Michael Garroutte
Senior Investigator, Martin Investigative Services

As I close out this discussion on divorce, I'd like to discuss a very important aspect of keeping families safe, healthy, and well. We spend so much time protecting ourselves, our homes, and our children from outsiders, when often the trouble lies inside, with those closest to us.

Certain things stick with you from a seminary education in the late sixties. One of them is the sanctity of home, hearth, and marriage. In other words: *No Divorce*. As a Catholic, I accepted this edict unquestioningly. After years of conducting marital surveillance for a primarily female clientele, my opinions on divorce began to change. Radically. Over and over I saw women who were staying in terrible relationships—though granted, anyone consulting me was already on the marital *Titanic*.

"OK, Mary Lou," I would ask. "Are you in an abusive relationship?" The women would always say, "Oh no, my husband would never hit me." Sigh. "Let me ask again . . . are you in an abusive relationship?" "No, I just told you I wasn't," they would reply, somewhat perplexed.

"Well, you think he's cheating on you. How does he treat you other-wise . . . what's the worst thing he's ever said to you? Or the worst name he's ever called you?"

"Oh, he calls me all kinds of names; I'm too embarrassed to tell you some of the things he's said."

"Do you understand that that verbal abuse can be as damaging to you as physical abuse . . . even more harmful sometimes . . . because it doesn't leave any marks? That doesn't mean the damage to your soul and self-esteem isn't devastating." Sometimes I got through, more often I did not. I saw countless husbands who cheated. Verbally and/or physi-cally abused the wife and kids. Drank or gambled away the rent money. Did drugs. Vanished for days at a time. There came a point where I had to wonder . . . what does it take to make these women toss these bums out?

The first time I actually asked this question, a bright, beautiful young woman sat across from me. Her husband regularly smacked her around, and I'd just gotten proof that he was cheating on her as well. She was waffling about what to do next. I couldn't take seeing yet another reac-tion like this. She deserved so much better than what she had. The words just flew out of my mouth in frustration. "You're going to stay with this guy? Is this really the best you can do?"

She reared back in her chair, her eyes wide open. She came right back at me with an indignant, "No! Of course not." My question to her then, and to countless others like her since that day: What are you going to do about it? You've got forty or fifty more years on this planet, do you plan to spend them living like this?

I like to believe I've become more patient and diplomatic as I've gotten older, but when I was younger it was a real struggle not to burst out with, "What is wrong with you?" on a near-daily basis. I remember blurting out, "Even Jesus got really angry, not once but twice, and threw the money-changers out of the temple. Maybe you could tap into a little of that righteous anger?" I couldn't understand why so many smart, good-looking women would allow themselves to stay in some of the situations they found themselves in. I concluded that the answer is fear. For many people, the fear of the unknown is greater than the discomfort of the current arrangement.

I began to believe that in many cases my job was to give some women I was seeing the confidence to start moving away from the man they married . . . something that went against all my original training and instincts. By a certain point, many clients became completely beaten down. By the time they found themselves watching video of a cheating spouse while sitting across from me, their self-esteem had pretty much vanished; all they could do was offer weak excuses.

"I'm going to stay for the children," is one excuse that I no longer buy at all. That is a great way to set a terrible example, ruin their childhoods, and set them up for their own troubled relationships later in life. Most kids these days by the age of ten know more than I did the day I graduated from seminary school. Come on, with all the social media and information on the Internet? Don't kid yourself. You're not doing children any favors by sticking around in a toxic marriage. My best advice when it comes to any type of abuse is: Don't stay for your kids. *Leave* for your kids. Especially when it's an abusive situation.

"He says he's going to change" is another phrase I've heard a million times. Please take it from me, you're not going to change any man. As someone who has been involved in thousands of divorce cases, I've yet to see any woman ever change a man. Oh, I've seen plenty of men put on quite a tap dance for a few months to win someone back . . . sure. But that's never enough. A leopard generally doesn't change its spots.

Since 1970 the divorce rate has increased by 40 percent. Far from decrying this trend, I now view the epidemic of how long some people will stay together when they shouldn't as more of a tragedy. I can't even imagine what the divorce rate would be if so many women weren't so forgiving and stayed with guys they shouldn't for so long. I sincerely root for happy, rewarding lives for all my clients and try to help them attain that in the here and now. Don't wait for your reward in heaven!

The biggest mistake women make when divorcing involves what they did during their marriage, not during the divorce. As a family law attorney practicing in Southern California for over twenty-nine years, I represent both men and women. With respect to many of the women, what I see happening is somewhat surprising. Although we are now well into the twenty-first century, the reality is there are still many married women who fail to become self-supporting or even make any effort to become self-supporting until their divorce.

I personally have been married for twenty-eight years and am in my mid-fifties, the same age as many of my clients. This group, along with so many of my contemporaries, are not only financially dependent upon their husbands, they also have no knowledge or understanding of the financial issues in their own household. These women are what family law lawyers call the "out" spouse, the one who's in the dark about money and property, with zero control of or even access to financial information or resources. This is not a good place to be.

Where there is an "out" spouse, the husband and wife are not equal partners. They never were. Yes, they may have children together, and they may make joint decisions about schooling, religion, discipline, and the like. But when it comes to financial matters, many women abdicated that responsibility from day one. They're OK being in the dark, because they're OK with being taken care of. They say, "If I had told my husband when we got engaged that I needed to be a signer on all the accounts and be involved in all financial decisions, there would have been hell to pay. Our relationship wouldn't have survived; we probably wouldn't have gotten married." This should have been a giant red flag right from the start. Unfortunately, the marriage didn't survive and now there's hell to pay.

What we're talking about is essentially a parent-child relationship when it comes to finances. The husband is in charge of making and doling out money. The wife lives on an allowance, just like we all did as kids growing up. It's very old-fashioned, but still quite prevalent. These marriages run by what I like to call the other Golden Rule: He who makes the gold, makes the rules. Women are willing to accept this arrangement because they don't want to rock the boat or create conflict . . . not to mention, they're usually busy making a home and raising children (which is a very important full-time job that for some unknown reason neither husband nor wife believes entitles the woman to equal input or access to money or financial information). Instead, she must depend upon her "knight in shining armor" to take care of her and the children in every way (until he doesn't).

What these women don't appreciate is that the balance of power is so uneven. If they stay married to one spouse all of their lives until one or the other passes away, OK, no harm, no foul. But this is a world where there is a significant divorce rate. In a marriage where this financial disparity exists and then there's a divorce, they are at risk to be crushed.

A divorce generally goes the same way the marriage did. There are plenty of women out there who have their own careers, earn their own money, and maintain an equal financial partnership with their spouses. Those divorces go quite a bit differently than those of the "out" spouses. It's pretty simple: women who are at risk to get run over in a divorce (without the right representation) are the same women who got run over in the marriage!

When it's time to divorce, the "out" wives simply have no idea what's going on. They don't have their name on the bank accounts, their credit cards are shut off, and they have to file with the court to request support because they have no access to money. These motions take time. It's not an overnight process. Meanwhile, they are in dire financial straits. Sometimes we can get opposing counsel to convince the husband to give his estranged wife some of the community money from the start. More often she has to borrow from friends or family members to retain an attorney and to put food on the table until a support order is entered. These are marriages that have failed, after all. People are not generally kind and loving toward each other during this process. As a result, what was once standard operating procedure during the marriage (being supported like a child) becomes an outrageous punitive tactic during the divorce (being treated like a child with no allowance). Keep in mind, this is community money, but she doesn't have access to it because she never did.

A woman in this situation must hire an attorney who is a warrior, someone who will fight for her and stand up for her in a way that didn't happen in the marriage. This is the first step in leveling a playing field that has been wildly unequal for years, usually decades. The wheels of justice turn slowly, as they say. Balancing these scales until she gets her fair share of the pie can, and usually does, take a very long time, a huge amount of work, and a great deal of money.

Most of these women have lived very pleasant, affluent lives for a long time. If they divorce, they feel it is a badge of honor to receive spousal support. They're entitled to it; someone has to pay for their lifestyle. I can't tell you how many times I've heard, "This was a long-term marriage; I'm entitled to lifetime spousal support, right?" The answer is, *Yes but*. . . . You need it and will get it at the beginning, but to rely upon it long term is very risky. I try to educate these women that this is not something to count on for the rest of their lives. Men die, suffer business reversals, retire, and/or hide their money, just to name a few things that can seriously jeopardize long-term support.

So yes, they may be entitled to lifetime spousal support . . . but sometimes "lifetime" is only two to five years. That's the amount of time that generally passes before the ex-spouse is back in court, trying to modify the support order, complaining that business is down and that he's no longer making money, etc., etc. Sometimes he wins, sometimes he doesn't, but I hate to see women continue to depend upon their ex-husbands for their financial well-being. It's just too risky. It's not going to carry the day until they die, just like their marriage didn't carry the day till the end!

What really matters when divorcing is how much of a pie has been created during the marriage. Hopefully, the wife's share is enough to live on for the rest of her life. If not, it's like starting over late in life when abilities and opportunities may not be what they once were. The husband, on the other hand, gets his half of the pie and retains his earning capacity. He will move on and continue to live the lifestyle he has become accustomed to, while she lives off of diminishing property, modifiable support that he keeps chipping away at, or earnings from a menial job because her earning capacity was never maximized before or during the marriage. The likelihood of her maintaining the marital lifestyle on spousal support alone is very small, except in cases of truly tremendous wealth. Even in those cases, it is better for women to get what is called a spousal buyout, a large tax-free lump sum instead of monthly payments. Who wants to be running to the mailbox every month looking for their check? And what happens when it's late or not there at all? Spousal support is not a guaranteed annuity. And if it comes from a self-employed, disgruntled ex-husband, the ex-wife is just another low-priority creditor at his mercy.

Still, many women want a property settlement and monthly spousal support and to be "supported." There are many times we get all the way to the end of a divorce—everything has been settled, the pie has been divided, support is being paid or bought out—and my client will say to me, "He's still going to pay my health insurance and car payment, right?" Wrong. New lifestyle. New life. You're going to be a grownup and pay your own car payment from now on, whether that's out of your settlement, your support, or your new job.

Facing this reality is not something that happens overnight. While being an advocate for these women during the divorce, a big part of my job is educating and encouraging women to become financial grownups. To pay their own bills, get educated, and ultimately achieve financial independence. This is a huge challenge. After all, these women have been birds in a cage, and when a cage has been absolutely beautiful and gilded, or when the bird has been told for years she couldn't survive outside the cage, many are reluctant to leave it. However, beautiful or not, it is still a prison and it's liberating to leave it! Once freed, they no longer need to ask their husband's permission for anything. They are finally in charge of their own destiny for the first time.

Many of these women rise to the occasion wonderfully, because they have to. Despite the pain of divorce, emancipation can be an incredibly empowering process. I know because I have seen many birds fly high once the divorce is over.
Jacqueline A. Whisnant, Partner
Phillips Whisnant Gazin Gorczyca and Curtin, LLP
Newport Beach, California

4

LOVE IS A CON

A beautiful woman walked into my office and said, "I need your help." Sounds like the opening to every PI story you've ever heard, right? It was actually the beginning of the end for Colum McCall,[1] con man extraordinaire. He cut quite a swath through Orange County in the early nineties. He is the perfect cautionary tale of a situation I've seen played out too many times to count: conned in the name of love.

Olivia, my new client, was having second thoughts about her boyfriend. Colum McCall was a former pro golfer and an extremely handsome man. He was also an investment advisor who guaranteed a tenpercent return on her money. A self-made businesswoman, Olivia was quite wealthy in addition to being stunning. However, she'd been in a bad car accident the year before and now needed permanent leg braces that were bulky and unsightly. Her health and confidence had taken quite a hit, which put her in quite a susceptible position.

Olivia had given a hefty sum of money to her new guy but almost immediately regretted it. Something didn't feel right; she was afraid she had been swindled. I like to solve problems quickly. I didn't see any need for lots of investigation or surveillance. In a situation like this, I am always in favor of calling the "advisor" up and saying, "My client wants her money back . . . and I am here to make sure she gets it, in a cashier's check, now." Let him go steal money from someone or somewhere else to get the cash . . . I don't really care. I just want to make my client whole again. That's my job. I called Colum, and he agreed to see me.

---

1. Pseudonym has been used to protect identity.

Colum had one hell of a line. It was easy to see how he could charm the ladies. "Listen, what are you doing?" I asked him as we sat at a back table in a small, out-of-the-way restaurant. "Taking advantage of this poor incapacitated woman at this vulnerable time in her life?" This was a man accustomed to being able to talk his way out of anything. He was well aware that I was an investigator working for Olivia, but, like many con artists, he was completely confident in his powers of persuasion. He freely told me everything, man to man, thinking he could win me over to his side.

He explained his modus operandi. He would drive around Newport in his Rolls-Royce looking for women in expensive late-model cars holding cell phones. He'd track their car until he pulled alongside them at a stoplight, get their attention and say, "Give me your number, or I'll give you mine; I'd love to take you out sometime." He might do this twenty times a day . . . all he needed was one hit. If they bit, he wined and dined them and told them he was a retired professional golfer who managed investments. Pretty soon, he got them to hand over money.

As we talked I couldn't believe the depth of the con. He currently had *nine* "girlfriends" on the string. All of them educated, accomplished women who had achieved great financial success. They were gifting him with jewelry, cars, and hundreds and hundreds of thousands of dollars to "invest." That's a huge income, granted, but juggling nine women and keeping them happy? Now that really is a professional.

I walked out of the meeting shaking my head. I soon had eight more women clamoring to become my client. I took them all on, gathered their information, put everything together into one detailed report, and headed over to a local police department. "There's a con man out there, and this is what he's done," I told the detective. "He has committed felonies. It's all right here for you in black and white." I handed over my work product, and very shortly I heard from a detective, who appreciated all the work I had done for them. "This is great," he told me. "We'd like you to call him and set up another meeting."

You'd think a meeting with Colum would take place at a ritzy Newport Beach restaurant with the ocean and yachts in the background. In reality, we met at a Carl's Jr. on a Saturday morning, which made it much easier for the cops to blend in. My sign to the police was that when I took my pen out of my pocket, it was time to swoop in. The second I reached into my jacket pocket, eight officers materialized out of nowhere and *boom!* They took Colum down, handcuffed him, and carted him off to jail.

Here's the best part: Olivia, my original client, called me to say, "I'm not going to testify against him. I'm going to marry him." And she did. When all was said and done, she simply refused to accept that she was just another con to him. The judge at his trial didn't care who either one of them married or why and sent Colum to jail for two years. Before he went off to serve his time, I managed to recover a decent amount of money and property from him and have it returned to the other eight women. He began serving his time, and I returned to investigating.

Several months later I was sitting in my office when I got a call from the Oprah show. "We're calling about this case of the pro golfer con man. . . . We hear there's a movie coming out about it, and we'd like to have you and some of the women on the show." The movie rumor turned out to be true. The late, great TV producer Stephen J. Cannell was making a made-for-TV movie about Colum. Their office eventually reached out to me as well.

All eight women were very excited when I initially called. Oprah! Arrangements were made for three of my clients and me to fly in and tape the show in Chicago. But when my clients eventually realized they were going to be on national TV, in front of her huge audience, to tell the world, pretty much, what trusting, blind fools they had been, they all backed out. I had been so excited . . . I was packed and ready to go with my brand-new shirt and tie. "Hey, don't worry, I'll still come on the show!" I told the producer. "Ummm. . . . No thank you," I was told.

✸ ✸ ✸

You might wonder . . . how could so many smart, sophisticated women be taken in by what, in retrospect, is such an obvious con man? After three decades in business, all I can say is that many otherwise savvy adults, both men and women, fall for all kinds of things . . . mainly because they want so badly to believe that they've won money, been offered a can't-miss investment, or the exciting man or woman of their dreams has finally arrived. In fact, a not-infrequent request in my line of work is from clients wanting to confirm whether or not their significant other is a Navy SEAL or an agent with the Central Intelligence Agency (CIA).

Most of these inquiries come from wives and girlfriends, attempting to uncover where their husbands disappear to on their supposed clandestine business trips or secret rendezvous. Let me spell this out as clearly as I can: If your significant other claims to be a CIA agent, I guarantee you that he or she most certainly is not. The likelihood that your spouse is a "secret agent" is right up there with the likelihood of you winning the lottery—twice.

In more than thirty years as a private investigator, I have never once verified that someone's spouse or partner is actually in the CIA, a SEAL, or any kind of "secret agent," for that matter. Not once. If you want to run a background check on somebody, great. If your new boyfriend tells you he's a spy doing classified work, or a Navy SEAL, and you're looking for confirmation, please don't waste your time or money. Just trust me—he isn't.

So when do I think a background check is warranted? If you're middle-aged and getting married, this is very likely the second trip down the aisle for you and your intended (or even the third). It is also likely that you've both accumulated some assets along the way. All divorce records in the United States are available; they are a matter of public record. It's a big red flag if someone won't tell you in what county or state their divorce was finalized. That's generally because they don't want you to see the official record. I always recommend that everyone read their fiancé's divorce file . . . if for no other reason than you can see what they'll someday say about you. I'm kidding! But truly, it's best to know if there were drug or abuse allegations thrown around. Anyone with nothing to hide should be happy to share those details.

The main thing to keep in mind is that the IRS loves it when people get married! All of your intended's assets and liabilities will soon be officially yours as well. If he or she has liens or judgments, as a legally wed spouse, you are now fair game. There's nothing the IRS likes better than to attach a new bank account. Wherever there's a lot of money at stake, a background investigation, prenup, and discussions with a lawyer before the wedding are all in order.

If there is one running theme throughout this book—just one piece of advice I would like to get through to readers—it's that an ounce of prevention is worth a pound of cure. Love is wonderful; marriage is a business deal. Find out about any unpleasant surprises *before* you walk down the aisle!

* * *

Now, I'm no expert on love affairs conducted in prisons, but I do believe the general public is a bit naïve in terms of not realizing a) how incredibly manipulative criminals can be and b) just how far a prisoner will go to achieve his ends. This sort of thing is far more common than people realize.

In the summer of 2015, the country was riveted by news of a prison break from the Clinton Correctional Facility in upper New York. Convicted murderers David Sweat and Richard Matt escaped from their adjoining cells in maximum security, leaving a taunting note with a smiley face and the words "Have a Nice Day" behind. They managed to evade authorities for three long weeks before finally being cornered after a massive manhunt. Matt was killed in the ensuing shootout; Sweat was critically wounded but survived to be taken back into custody.

It was clear the pair had had some inside help escaping. Married correctional officer Joyce Mitchell, who had supervised the men in the prison machine shop, admitted to smuggling power tools to the friends. It soon emerged that she had been romantically involved with Matt, and the original plan was for her to drive the pair to safety in a getaway car before she chickened out at the last minute. After it was all over, Joyce sat for an interview, wearing a striped jail uniform and handcuffs. The chastened fifty-one-year-old mother could only say that she had gotten in over her head. Matt Lauer wondered whether she had been controlled by Matt. "Yes," she responded wanly, "he was good at that."

These guys are street smart; they instinctively hone in on those who are easy to manipulate. A law-abiding average female citizen who is often a bit idealistic and has a true desire to help? Trust me, these guys will say or do anything to win her over . . . *anything*. A volunteer or teacher or worker in a prison still leaves every night; they have a life and responsibilities when they head home. A prisoner has twenty-four hours a day in which to plot, plan, and focus solely on how to win someone over. Particularly in the case of a woman not accustomed to much male attention, the experience can be overwhelming. And of course it always starts with one baby step.

The prisoner is attentive, polite, and respectful. Grateful for whatever time someone spends with him. A friendly relationship starts to develop. It starts to become just a bit warmer than strictly proper, with maybe just a touch of flirting. Then comes a small request . . . something as innocuous as "Hey, can you get me a candy bar?" "I can't do that, it's against the rules!" is the woman's first response. But as time goes on, the rules begin to seem silly, and soon she's buying the candy bar. Fast-forward a few months, and she's giving her lover drawings of the prison plans so he can bust out and they can be together forever.

Don't get me wrong, there are many wonderful people in the world who do good deeds for the less fortunate, and that includes prisoners. However, this is a love con of the worst kind. Please remember, most of these people are incarcerated for a reason, and exercise caution and good judgment!

※ ※ ※

Finally, in terms of love cons, here is the number one scam I see all the time. There is not a day that goes by in my office—in fact, I would say we get at least ten inquiries a week—from a prospective female client who is active on Internet dating sites. A word of caution: Predators know where to find prey. Scammers of elderly people, trying to scare victims into sending money by saying they're from the IRS or Medicare, are going to target Florida, California, and Arizona—states with three of the largest populations of retirees. To a con artist, dating sites are a huge pool of single women/potential marks putting themselves out there, looking for love, sometimes a little too willing to suspend disbelief and common sense.

The purpose of these calls is to ask us to verify whether a man she has been corresponding with, or "dating," over the Internet is actually who his profile says he is. She wants to be sure, for example, that the person e-mailing, texting, and calling her really is John Smith, divorced accountant, who lives in Lake Forest, Illinois.

My first question is always, "Have you sent him money?" If the answer is "No," then I'm happy. It means that there's something I can do. Hopefully, there's actually a real guy out there I can check out and whatever is going on might even lead to a real relationship. That would be great. But I am always prepared for an affirmative answer, which means my next question is "How much?" I've heard everything from a defensive "Just a little," or "A couple hundred bucks," all the way up to a worried, "I've sent him $180,000."

When I ask the women what in the world got them to send money, the lines are ridiculous. These men say things like: I'd love to come see you; send me a changeable first-class ticket from New York to Los Angeles because my schedule's so unpredictable right now. The woman does, only to hear: My kid needs surgery. My brother's got leukemia. I'll get out to see you as soon as I possibly can! Of course nobody ever shows up. This is just one of the hundreds of ways con artists extract money from the many, many women they have on the hook.

Again, I know it's hard to believe smart people actually fall for this stuff, but they do, much more often than you'd think. Pursue a hundred females online, and one or two will absolutely fall for your story, no matter how many red flags. It's nothing more than a numbers game!

I am all for dating and finding love, but I would like to once again urge caution when it comes to any online relationship. Don't wait until after the fact to investigate, because it's very difficult to recoup large sums of money, even with a first-class private eye helping. Most of it, sadly, has disappeared into places like Russia or Nigeria, lost forever behind endless untraceable fake accounts.

There's a reason why all the calls I get are about long-distance relationships. Let's say you live in the Chicago area . . . surely you can at least start by dating people in the state of Illinois, whom you can easily meet in person? Set up some dates with actual people, not whoever might be behind a screen name thousands of miles away. Resolve to start dating locally . . . and never, ever send money! At this stage of the game, "love" should not cost a thing!

I was twenty-six years old when I entered Basic Underwater Demolition/SEAL (BUDS) training, which is certainly at the older end of the spectrum. I took my time and did my research about the requirements. At that time the US Navy offered what was called the Dive Fare program. The idea was that you could enlist in the navy, try out for BUDS, and if you didn't make the cut, you could get right back out of the navy. They started to lose too many recruits that way, so the program changed. The process I went through was a bit tougher. When I entered boot camp, I was guaranteed a shot at BUDS. I would take the physical tests necessary to be allowed to enter training; if I passed, I could go.

If I made it through BUDS and became a Navy SEAL, I would owe the navy two extra years on my enlistment—this is, I would serve a six-year hitch instead of the regular four. If I didn't make it, I would have to serve a four-year hitch in the regular navy. I didn't particularly want to be in the navy, but you have to be in the navy to be a SEAL. Obviously. Once I made it into BUDS, I was very highly motivated to stay in, because I didn't want to get bumped back down to the regular navy.

I would say that any documentaries or reality shows you may have seen about "The Making of a SEAL" were probably pretty good, but take my word for it, they're toned down. They have to be for television. Instructors who know they're on camera are going to be a bit more . . . *civil* might be the best word. It's a pretty significant ramp-up in terms of physical exercise and mental stress for most people. You get shin splints, stress fractures—all kinds of injuries that happen under stress.

I had prepared pretty well for the calisthenics end of things—sit-ups, push-ups, exercises like that. I certainly wished I had done more running. In hindsight, I would have run farther, faster, and on a more regular basis, as that quickly proved to be my weakest spot. And it was certainly a weakness the instructors could make me pay for. On land, it's easy to make guys do extra laps, running, fireman carries, whatever they decide. They have all kinds of "games" to play when you're on the slow side; that extra punishment hurt.

But here's the thing: in the end, if you do what they tell you to do, pass your physical challenges, and don't quit, the six months passes and you're done. It's really just a matter of not getting hurt; injuries set a lot of guys back. Mostly, a lot of people quit. That's just a fact, and that's fine, because it's far better to quit in the training environment than a real-life situation. Some guys get targeted because they come across as too cocky and draw too much attention to themselves. The majority of those guys learn their lesson fast. Certain guys are just naturally good at everything. Many just keep their heads down and try to get through it. But I stress: No one can make you quit. They can get on you and harass you to the point that you say, "Screw this, I quit," but that's ultimately your decision. Meet your times, pass your requirements, you will get through.

I lived in San Diego at the time I was going through training, and it was pretty common when I used to go out with friends in Pacific Beach at night to hear guys in bars spouting off about BUDS or being a SEAL. At some point, they'd learned enough about the process by trying for it themselves, having a friend or relative go through the program, or just by soaking up the military culture in the area. They knew enough to sound halfway legit, especially to someone who knows nothing about it.

We saw a bunch of guys who had failed out of BUDS and wound up somewhere else, but got far enough along so they had T-shirts from their class, or Hell Week, and they'd wear them around the bars to impress people. When pressed, some offered the excuse that they got hurt during training and were forced to drop out, which of course happens, just not as often as people claim. Most of the time they quit, wear their shirts around, and let people assume they're a full-blown SEAL team member.

Look, guys are guys, that's just kind of standard guy behavior. There are many, many kinds of men who want to be a part of that military community and contribute to that kind of discussion. That's not just for SEALs, but Army Rangers, Green Berets, and CIA officers, among many other groups. I personally just let this stuff go; people lie about things and misrepresent themselves all the time. They shouldn't, of course, but it is what it is.

I went into the navy late, served as a SEAL, left the navy, and then got into the fire department late. Firefighter is my lifetime career; currently, I am a captain in the Los Angeles Fire Department. Certainly, having been a SEAL gives you a bit of perspective on things for the rest of your life. When you're a military employee, the government really pretty much owns you and controls every aspect of your life, for the most part. Even though the fire department or law enforcement are somewhat paramilitary organizations, you can walk away at any time. That was not an option in the military.

Of course, bad days working in the fire department can be very bad. They might involve tragedy, loss of property and lives, the deaths of good friends and colleagues. That can happen, and that's like the SEALs. But we train hard to prevent as much of that kind of outcome as we can. On both jobs. The fire department is a great job, but it's not something I want to do forever either. For one thing, the body just doesn't hold up forever in these kinds of professions.

These days, my wife and I work in the real estate company we founded. I stay in touch with some of my former SEAL buddies, some in person, some in a private Facebook group we all belong to. Sometimes one of the guys will say something like, "This guy so-and-so said he was in here at this time . . . " and someone else will get back to him saying, "Yes, I know him," or "No, he's full of it." We also see a lot of photographs scrolling through Facebook with guys all dressed up in a uniform, with all their medals in the wrong spot; the trident is on the wrong side; all kinds of extra stuff that shouldn't be there. Sometimes guys even get our address and post these pictures up on our group page for all of us to see.

There is an actual official list out there of every person who has ever gone through BUDS training. It's not public record, but it's certainly not impossible to access. There are former SEALs who do name checks on a pretty regular basis; they take a strong interest in those who claim to be something they're not. As I said, it doesn't really upset me. Other SEALs feel differently!

Mark McCracken

Ex-Navy SEAL

5

SCAMS AND SUCKERS

Specifically, I wrote this book because I want to raise awareness that there are some great private investigators at work in this country. These men and women have the power to change lives for the better in many ways most people have never even considered. More generally, I would really like to see Mr. and Mrs. John Q. Public simply become more aware of what's going on around them and encourage them to raise their defenses a little bit higher. So many people are running all kinds of games, trying to gain an advantage however they can. Here's my rule of thumb: Everybody's guilty until proven innocent!

Not to be cynical, just realistic: There are very few Mother Teresas out there. The last time the Catholic Church canonized saints, they found only two, out of the billions of people who have lived on this earth. There is no benevolent stranger out there ready to pick up the phone this week to call (or send you an e-mail) for the express purpose of giving you something. Let's be real: Have you ever gotten a call from any stranger, in your life, who simply wanted to deposit money into your bank account? Or hand you something of value for nothing?

I am quite sure you have not. However, there is no end to the scam artists out there who promise every kind of something for nothing. With the maturity of the Internet came the maturity of the online scam artist. Now there are more cons than ever before. It's easy for thieves to steal identities, obtain personal information, and leech money from you and the people you love. Unfortunately, we live in the golden age of the con artist.

But let's go back a decade or so, when the Internet was still in its infancy. On the surface, Mary Winkler and her husband Matthew shared an idyllic small-town life in Tennessee. He was a handsome, dynamic young preacher at Church of Christ; she was a devoted wife and mother to their three young girls. The couple had fallen in love in college and by all accounts were devoted to each other for the first years of their marriage. The stress of supporting a growing family on his small salary led to growing unhappiness on both their parts. Some friends and family members would later claim that Matthew had a critical, controlling nature, which heightened the tension in their home.

Mary awoke early one morning in the spring of 2006, fetched her husband's shotgun from their closet and shot him in the back as he lay in bed. The bullets shattered his spine and tore through his internal organs. He fell off the bed and, as Mary would later tell officials, asked her "Why?" as he choked on his own blood. This was the question on everyone's mind as they struggled to understand what could have driven this shy, quiet mother to such violence. It soon emerged that being victimized by a scam had certainly contributed to the young mother's troubles.

Investigators learned that some months before Mary had opened a letter that landed in their mailbox and promised huge cash rewards. The letter included a foreign check for $6,500, which Mary promptly deposited and wrote checks against as directed in the letter. The check was fraudulent, but the hook had been set. Mary soon got a post office box to keep all mail away from her husband and then opened five separate checking accounts in neighboring towns where she transferred sums in an increasingly frantic shuffle to stay afloat. She was waiting for the big payoff that, of course, would never come.

After several months, the jig was up. One of the banks she was defrauding in what had become a complicated check-kiting scam ran out of patience. They pressured Mary to come in for a meeting to resolve the situation. They also advised her to bring her husband. The bank set the deadline for March 22—the very day Matthew was shot. Prosecutors at her murder trial detailed the arguments the couple had had over finances for months, leading to an especially heated fight the night before his death. Mary was so angry at her husband, they claimed, and so afraid of his wrath once he discovered how deeply she had mired them in debt, that she killed him rather than face him . . . and the bank officers.

The case became a national sensation when Mary's attorneys used the battered-wife defense and elicited lurid testimony about the sexual demands her husband had supposedly placed on her. There was even more of an uproar when Mary was eventually convicted of voluntary manslaughter but served only seven months in custody—two of those months in a mental health facility. She emerged to resume her quiet life in Tennessee and eventually regained custody of her three daughters. Certainly, there was much hidden behind the couple's closed doors that will never be known, but there is no doubt falling prey to ruthless con artists helped push a desperate woman over the edge.

A letter in the mailbox started the "advance check" scam that helped destroy the Winklers and thousands of other naïve families. This con, in which prizes or gifts are promised and include a check with directions to pay fees or wire money to third parties, sounds almost quaint these days. However, the more things change, the more they stay the same. Many of the most popular cons going on today are merely updated versions of time-tested ways to separate the gullible from their money.

✦ ✦ ✦

Face to face, over the phone, or via e-mail, the strong-arm approach uses the power of intimidation and/or hiding behind faux authority to make you fear for your freedom or personal/financial safety. For example, someone might call posing as an attorney and tell you that you need to pay a certain amount of money or face collections. They warn that you have no time to lose and that this is your last opportunity to settle an old and forgotten debt. Some people are intimidated enough to send a check or give out a credit card number.

Someone posing as a law enforcement officer might call to say that your grandson/brother/cousin has landed in jail and needs to be bailed out. The spiel goes something like this: "He's behind bars and not allowed to make phone calls. But he gave me your number, here's what needs to happen. You have to go down to Western Union or Money-Gram and send money to this particular station in the town where he's being held. His bail is $687."

These scams can be quite convincing, with the caller referencing the name and other details about your relative—something that is simple for anyone to find with even a cursory check of Facebook accounts. Someone pulled this one on my eighty-seven-year-old father once . . . he said, "Let my grandson rot in jail," and hung up. He was savvier than most, having run one of my offices for several years.

I imagine most readers would say to me that they, too, would never fall for this kind of thing. But take a million people . . . how many will fall for it? One percent? That's ten thousand victims who send money! Once again, it's a numbers game. Here's one of the latest—this one designed to strike fear into the heart of every American citizen. Let's say you're at home one afternoon making lunch when the phone rings. The caller ID display reads "IRS" and the phone number that shows up is the toll-free official number 800-829-1040. The brusque caller gets right to the point, stating that he/she is an IRS agent and saying that you owe them money.

This con tends to be particularly successful because nobody ever wants to run afoul of the IRS. The initial reaction is often just to pay whatever fee they say you owe and get the whole matter behind you before "penalties" and "interest" start accruing. The scammers who make these calls have evolved to the point they are able to spoof the caller ID information, when in reality the majority originate from foreign countries. This is why the fake "agents" are often so aggressive and demanding. They know they will never be caught.

At one point NBC Channel 4 in Los Angeles aired one of the many consumer warnings about IRS scams and included some of the calls that had been recorded by citizens. Here are just a few of the scare tactics the callers used to threaten them: filing liens on the house; garnishing paychecks; freezing and confiscating all bank accounts; deporting them; seizing their property. These are very potent threats.

The mother-in-law of a friend of mine was hit with a new version of the telephone tax scam this year. A call came in with "911" on the caller ID screen. The man on the line identified himself as being with the "San Diego Sheriff's Department" and asked if she had been informed that the IRS had filed a tax complaint against her. She hung up. The same person called right back and demanded to know why she hung up on an officer of the law. The man then told her that they were sending a unit to her address that afternoon to pick up the money that was owed. She hung up again. Of course no unit ever arrived.

The fear that that it "could be" a real IRS or law enforcement agent on the other end of the line often gives even the most law-abiding citizen pause. The promise that you can settle the issue today for $2,200 with a payment right now, versus $12,000 in fines and possible imprisonment down the road, leads many less than street-smart citizens "to do the deal." We've gotten quite a few calls saying, "Hey, I just sent $500 to the IRS . . . well, I'm pretty sure it was the IRS." Again, this is locking the barn door after the horse is stolen. That money is gone.

Almost every investigator at Martin Investigative Services is a former agent of the DEA, FBI, IRS, or Secret Service, and we know how they operate. Please know this for a fact: Hectoring phone calls is not how the IRS (or law enforcement) operates. IRS representative Lourdes Souss stresses, "The IRS would never threaten you. First of all, the IRS would never contact you by phone, or visit your house, or send you an email."[1] I urge readers to visit http://www.IRS.gov and click the "phishing and tax scams" button to read more about the latest creative ways scammers are taking advantage of taxpayers.

As far as all those ads you hear on the radio or see on TV and the Internet promising relief from IRS debt? The ones who say that you need someone tough on your side to go up against the IRS when you've fallen hopelessly behind? Please don't be taken in by the misleading idea that hiring one of these firms will intimidate an agent charged with collecting the money you owe. IRS agents employ many skilled collections agents and have the full power of government and the law on their side. Trust me, they are not about to roll over no matter who you hire.

As the old saying goes, there's nothing certain in life besides death and taxes. It's foolish to put your head in the sand or hope that your case will fall through the cracks. Should you find yourself in this situation, bite the bullet and reach out. A good tax preparer or CPA will accomplish the same goal these firms promise with a huge monetary savings to you, your family, and/or your business. Ask your tax preparer and/or consultant if they have previous experience in dealing with the IRS. If not, you can avail yourself of CPA referrals who can represent you at http://www.aicpa.org.

---

1. "Beware Bogus IRS Phone Solicitations for Money," ABC News. Thursday, August 14, 2014,http://abc7.com/news/beware-bogus-irs-phone-solicitations-for-money/261886/.

The process becomes even simpler if you choose to do everything yourself online. You are eligible to apply for an online payment agreement and plan if as an individual you owe less than $50,000, or as a business you owe $25,000 or less. If you do not meet these standards, there are other options: installment agreements, an offer in compromise (settling for less than the full amount, though I advise you not to spend too much time here), or temporarily delaying the collections process. Their site has a helpful section of what-if scenarios for struggling taxpayers. Go to http://www.IRS.gov and hit the "payments" tab.

Meanwhile, should you ever receive a random call from someone stating they are from the IRS or law enforcement collecting for the IRS, just hang up. The IRS will always open communications through old-fashioned snail mail if you owe them money. Meanwhile, you can report the call to the IRS at 800-829-1040, and file a complaint with the Federal Trade Commission (FTC), which only takes a few minutes.

✿ ✿ ✿

In these hyper-connected days, computer cons are by far the most popular and pervasive. Scammers can reach millions of people all over the world, instantly, with the click of a mouse. Instead of sending out actual letters or making phone calls, email is now the preferred method of outreach because it is (relatively) inexpensive to spam. Is there anyone, anywhere, with any kind of email account who has not been contacted by a deposed Nigerian prince? You know, the one graciously offering to transfer thirty million dollars into your account if you'll handle some minor banking tasks for him first?

Below is an example of one of the latest e-mail cons making the rounds; this one showed up in my own inbox. Again . . . the vast majority of people would delete it and never give it another thought. For those who are particularly naïve, or fearful, or troubled, I'm sad to say it might prove effective.

ATTENTION TOM: I FEEL SORRY FOR YOU. IT IS A PITY THAT YOUR LIFE IS GOING TO END SOON.

SOMEONE WHOM YOU CONSIDER A FRIEND WANTS YOU DEAD. THIS PERSON CAME TO US AND SAID THAT HE WANTED YOU DEAD. HE PROVIDED US WITH YOUR NAME, PHOTO AND OTHER NECESSARY INFORMATION WE NEEDED TO LOCATE YOU. THIS PERSON SPENT A LOT OF MONEY ON THIS VENTURE.

SO I SENT MY BOYS TO TRACK YOU DOWN. THIS INCLUDED THE BUGGING OF YOUR PHONE WITH SATELLITE TRACKING DEVICES. THEY HAVE NOW CARRIED OUT THE NECESSARY INVESTIGATION WE NEED FOR THE OPERATION ON YOU. IF YOU DOUBT THIS I WILL PROVIDE YOU WITH ALL THE INFORMATION WE HAVE GATHERED ABOUT YOU IN MY NEXT REPLY SO THAT YOU WILL SEE THAT I AM TELLING THE TRUTH.

MY DUTY IS JUST TO KILL YOU AS I HAVE ALREADY BEEN PAID FOR THAT. BUT I TOLD THEM NOT TO KILL YOU YET. I CALLED MY CLIENT BACK AND ASKED HIM FOR YOUR EMAIL ADDRESS, NOT SAYING WHAT I WANTED TO DO WITH IT. HE GAVE IT TO ME AND I AM CONTACTING YOU FIRST TO SEE IF YOUR LIFE IS IM-PORTANT TO YOU AND YOUR FAMILY. NOW . . . DO YOU WANT TO LIVE OR DIE?

ALL PLANS ARE IN PLACE TO KILL YOU. GET BACK TO ME NOW IF YOU ARE READY TO PAY SOME FEES TO SPARE YOUR LIFE. $8,000 IS ALL YOU NEED TO SPEND IN THIS PROCESS. YOU WILL FIRST OF ALL PAY $3,000, AND IN RETURN I WILL SEND A TAPE TO YOU. I RECORDED EVERY DISCUSSION I HAD WITH THE PERSON WHO WANTED YOU DEAD. AS SOON AS YOU RECEIVE THE TAPE, YOU WILL PAY THE REMAINING BALANCE OF $5,000.

IF YOU ARE NOT READY FOR MY HELP, THEN I WILL CARRY ON WITH MY JOB STRAIGHT-UP.

WARNING: DO NOT EVEN THINK OF CONTACTING THE POLICE OR EVEN TELL-ING ANYONE ABOUT THIS ARRANGEMENT, BECAUSE I WILL KNOW. YOUR CALLS AND EMAILS ARE BEING MONITORED. REMEMBER, SOMEONE CLOSE TO YOU WANTS YOU DEAD! WHEN I GIVE YOU THE TAPE OF ALL OUR DISCUSSIONS YOU CAN THEN USE IT TO TAKE ANY LEGAL ACTION. GOOD LUCK. I AWAIT YOUR REPLY. DO NOT DELAY!

A bit over the top, to be sure, but I'm sure it works on those who may have paranoid tendencies. Less cartoon-villain but scary in the opposite way, because of how very professional they are, is the latest computer scam I've seen going around involving cleaning a fake virus off new computers. I can't lie: I fell for this one myself.

I bought a new computer for my second home and had it all set up with the latest software installed. As I sat there typing one day I got an email saying . . . "Warning. Your new computer has been infected with the XYZ virus. Please call our toll-free number to speak to a representa-tive who will help you remove it." The email was professionally worded, and I succumbed to the very real fear that everyone who has just spent a couple grand on a new computer feels: that all their stuff could be wiped out. I called the number.

The "Microsoft rep" was smooth and professional. She asked me for some information and assured me that they would be able to wipe the virus from my computer. She sent me a link that I downloaded to help her "see" what the problem was. From that point on, she could tap into my computer from wherever she was. I watched in real time as she "cleaned" my hard drive, scoured my files, deleted "bugs" . . . whatever she claimed to be doing to "help" me. I had to pay $99, of course. The crazy thing was that I knew this had to be a scam, even as I watched someone going through all my files. The demonstration was amazing.

After nearly an hour, I finally said, "Are we done here?"

"Oh yes, absolutely, you should be fine from now on."

"Then listen closely. I know this is a scam. I am going to call my credit card company and contest this charge. I will not pay for it. You might as well reverse the charge right now, because I am not paying."

These people are pros; she didn't miss a beat. "Sir, are you not happy with the service we have provided? Because if you are not, we will not charge you." The people pulling this scam don't want any grief, or any scrutiny. Like I said, very smart.

"Why not review this work tonight and make sure there are no problems, and that there's nothing else we can do for you. I think you'll be happy with how everything works when we speak again tomorrow." She was still selling. She was so convincing that for a moment I hesitated again, honestly convinced that I really might have had a virus!

Then I came to my senses and insisted on the refund. They did reverse the charge on my credit card. All kinds of companies worldwide have agreements with the various computer manufacturers—IBM, Dell, Apple, all of the majors—to provide software. Somehow, hackers in India, South America, Russia—hell, they could be in Boston for all I know—have the ability to know that you have just bought a new computer. I've heard of this scam a bunch of times since it happened to me—it's especially popular among college students who freak out at the idea of something happening to their laptops.

Every day there's a new scam. I could never possibly stay on top of them. Nor can you. All I can do is encourage everyone to become a bit more aware, a bit less naïve, and a bit more questioning when people try to separate you from your money—whether that's in person, over the phone, or via e-mail.

* * *

Back in the bad old days, when New York was still gritty and crime-ridden, you couldn't walk more than a block from the train station before you'd see one of the oldest confidence tricks in history taking place on busy street corners. I am talking about three-card monte or the shell game, which in one form or another has been around since the Middle Ages. These masters of sleight of hand preyed on tourists; native New Yorkers knew that the dealer always wins. As a rule, big-city dwellers tend to be a bit more wary and alert to scams than the average person, which makes the following story all the more difficult to believe.

In the summer of 2013, a thirty-two-year-old British man named Niall was living in New York and working in marketing. After a stint in a rehab facility out west, he was back "home" at a loft in Williamsburg. Though he had begun to piece his life back together, he was sad and preoccupied. Niall had fallen hard for a fellow patient in rehab named Michelle. He was in love; Michelle did not return his feelings and made that very clear. Still, he could not forget her.

His lost love was on his mind one night as he walked through Times Square and on a whim stopped at a neon sign reading PSYCHIC in a storefront window. The young woman he met inside called herself Christina. She promised him that he and Michelle were meant to be together, and that she could bring Michelle back to him. Niall paid Christina $2,500 on this visit. It was to be the first of many.

For the next six months "Christina"—in actuality a con artist named Phyllis DeMarco, working with her husband, her "assistant," Bobby Evans—bled Niall dry. He spent a fortune on whatever she advised: diamonds to protect his energy, a "bridge" to trap evil spirits, and a "time machine" to clear his past—the time machine being a rose-gold Rolex watch for his psychic. At one point, he traveled to California to see Michelle, who once again pulled away from him. The rejection only caused Niall to redouble his efforts to win her back.

Hundreds of thousands of dollars and six months into this quest, Niall was stunned to see a notification on social media that Michelle had passed away. At this point, one would assume at least the con would end; it did not. Death was no problem for this psychic. First Christina told Niall that Michelle's death would only be real if he believed it to be. She then promised to reincarnate Michelle's spirit into the body of another woman, and encouraged Niall to go to Los Angeles to seek her out.

A year and a half after his first visit to a psychic, Niall had lost his apartment, savings, and car and was living on loans from friends and family. A "new" Michelle had not materialized. The final toll? Niall had been swindled out of more than $700,000. Niall was a wealthy, worldly executive—a far cry from naïve Mary Winkler in small-town Tennessee, for example. However, he was just as susceptible to a con artist when it came to getting what he wanted—in this case, love.

Here is the part of the story I find the most interesting: a private investigator saved the day. A year or so into his quest, Niall became suspicious of Christina and Bobby and did some research, which led him to PI Bob Nygaard, a specialist in scams involving psychics. Bob was the right man for the job: he remembered the couple from a previous scam they had run down in Florida. It was too late for him to save Niall's money, but he did compile an extensive report complete with bank statements and accompanied his client to the police station, where he handed over all the evidence. The couple was arrested, charged with grand larceny, and jailed.

Phyllis DeMarco and her husband were pros. They were running a con on steroids. Niall was an extreme example, of course, but I know so many people truly believe; it stuns me how many actually spend good money on this stuff. Psychics, mediums, healers, clairvoyants— whatever you call them—will read your palm, tell your future, align the stars, consult the tarot, burn a candle, cast a spell, remove a curse, bring you love, shower you with money . . . give them five hundred dollars and it will happen.

With all due respect to the psychics of the world, I just don't buy it. If someone wants to get their palm read at a fair or pay twenty bucks for a psychic reading I would say go ahead—if that's your idea of fun, then enjoy. At that level it's fairly harmless. But please don't take their "powers" seriously. I say this with great conviction because I've been involved with many psychics under the most serious circumstances imaginable.

On probably close to a couple hundred murder cases and missing persons investigations where the team worked with a psychic, I have yet to have even one truly help us or offer even a smidgen of actual evidence. The families of the victim are desperate; their loved one hasn't been seen for days, and they'll take any help they can get. I always listen to the psychic for ten minutes. Then I usually jump in to say . . . "Apart from all the smoke and mirrors, is there anything you have say to say that I can put into the E category?" They will ask, "What is the E category?" whereupon I say . . . "An evidence envelope."

"The body will be found near water," does not qualify as at "hit," as the earth is primarily made up of water. "The victim was most likely in a vehicle before they went missing . . . " doesn't either. "Anything more specific you might be able to tell us?" I always press them. There never is.

I believe that even if their motives are pure, the results are often harmful. These psychics are building up false hope in people who are exceptionally vulnerable. It's edging very close to one of the cruelest scams of all: claiming to have information about a missing person in order to collect a reward, get attention, or simply "troll" the suffering family. There's a special place in hell reserved for these people who prey upon those who have already been so beset. I don't even trust the psychics who offer to help for free; I believe they are trying to get publicity and align themselves with law enforcement agencies. They want to gain credibility by claiming they've worked with the San Francisco Police Department, for example.

James Randi was a brilliant magician and escape artist for decades. The heir apparent to Houdini retired from performing to become the foremost debunker of paranormal, pseudoscientific, and psychic scams in the entire world. The James Randi Educational Foundation (JREF) was founded in 1996 to "help people defend themselves from paranormal and pseudo-scientific claims."[2] For more than two decades, they offered a million-dollar prize to any psychic whose claims could withstand their scientific testing method. The rules of proof were simply what any legitimate experiment would require. To date, it has gone unclaimed. Their demonstrations of absolutely regular people—not psychics—doing "cold" readings on people who are astounded by their accuracy are pretty amazing too.

* * *

---

2. James Randi Educational Foundation, http://web.randi.org.

I mentioned earlier that my father, well into his eighties at the time, knew enough to hang up on a scammer trying to scare him into sending money. Having raised three sons with careers in law enforcement, and still in possession of all his marbles, he cut the caller off cold and never gave it another thought. Many others are not so lucky. A recent study in the *Journal of Internal Medicine* reported that approximately one in twenty seniors reported being financially abused in their later years. If this was a new disease, the journal noted, "a public health crisis would likely be declared."[3]

Seniors, of course, are ideal prey, as aging takes its toll on mental capabilities, being widowed leaves millions of men and women isolated and vulnerable, and loneliness makes them easy marks for "friendly" callers or visitors. The answer to this, of course, is watching out for them. The other day I made my biweekly visit to my father, who is still living alone in his home and going strong. He is a widower now; my mother lived in a facility briefly for a few weeks at the end of her life. We eventually decided to take her home, so she could pass in familiar surroundings with those she loved around her.

Still, those few weeks where she was in the care of strangers left quite an impression on me. I usually follow up seeing my father with a visit to one of the many senior homes in Orange County, ranging from a small bedroom in a modest private home to the most luxurious beachfront accommodations. The other day I dropped in unannounced for a quick visit with a good client's ninety-four-year-old mom. I asked her how she was sleeping, how her meals were, what she was doing with her day, and I took a peek around her room. Want to make an impression at your parent's retirement home? I guarantee you that a licensed PI visit will separate your mom and dad from the pack of residents. It takes me less than twenty minutes and does the resident a world of good.

When I walk into a facility and say, "Hi, I'm Tom Martin, and I'm a private investigator. I'm here to check on Mary Lou Smith," the reaction is priceless, and very telling. Some immediately get flustered and literally hold up their hands in front of me, as if to try to bar me. "Whoa, whoa, whoa . . . "

"There's no whoa here," I tell them politely. "I am giving you the courtesy of informing you that I am here to check on her welfare. I am

---

3. Salvatore, Diane. "Lies, Secrets and Scams: How to Prevent Elder Abuse." *Consumer Reports*, November 2015.

going to her room now. Thank you." And off I go. Sometimes with staffers in hot pursuit, nurses following along . . . all kinds of commotion. On those occasions when employees are flustered and scrambling, or immediately inform security that I'm there and try to block me from the residents' wing, I am pretty sure everything is not okay. Sometimes they give me a speech about protocol or privacy or whatever . . . but what if this was my own mother? Would I not be allowed just to walk in and see her unannounced whenever I wanted? I always think of her when I conduct these inspections or interview the occupants of the facility.

Sometimes a staff member will say, "We'd like to welcome you, Mr. Martin! Let's go find Mrs. Smith and see how she's doing today," and hold out their hand to me. That's when I know that these people are running a first-class facility. They are on top of their game and doing things right. It is always a delight to report good news to families. I like to say that I saw their father, who was happily playing cards, at a physical therapy class, eating a good meal, or simply resting in a comfortable chair in his room. Looking and feeling good. I regret having to make the other kind of call.

On one visit a couple of months ago, I found a client's mother at the end of a quiet hallway, sitting in a wheelchair and facing the wall. A nurse who had just come on duty came over and quietly informed me that the patient was in the same position where she'd been "parked" when the nurse left her previous shift eighteen hours earlier. No one had even checked on this resident or spoken to her since.

Is this the way someone's mother or sister is going to spend their last days on this earth? Alone and neglected? The incident sickened me. I read an article once about the fact that many Americans treat their pets with more care and regard than they do the senior citizens in their family. This is not an exaggeration. It is a reality. The only thing more upsetting than seeing this kind of neglect is when I make a call to the family about incidents like the one I've just described. It is very distressing to have a relative, son, or daughter say distractedly, "Oh thanks for checking on that Tom, I'll deal with it later." Or, "Gosh, OK, I'll get over there this week to check on her. Next week at the latest."

Good care is not expensive . . . it's priceless. We will all be seniors ourselves one day. Do not become one of these statistics in your later years. Start early, people—by middle age, at least—and get your long-term disability home care insurance in order. Don't count on anyone to watch out for you; do all you can to protect yourself now, while you still can. Your golden years are precious . . . prevent yourself from being victimized.

I am an attorney in private practice who has seen just about every kind of scam one could possibly imagine. When it comes to the age-old question, "Why do smart people fall for such pie-in-the-sky nonsense?" I find it helpful to reframe the question a bit. It's not so much about "smart" or "dumb"; I prefer to think of it as "greedy" versus "not greedy." I don't mean greed in the absolute worst sense of the word, but as a general rule, people are always looking to get something the easy way as opposed to the hard way. Slow, steady compound interest isn't good enough; they want to make 30, 40, 50 percent a year. Who's got twenty-five years to build up their estate? People want money, lots of it, right now.

To be honest, most people are just mentally lazy. Most successful people are very good at what they do to make their living. But when it comes to investments, they simply refuse to do their homework. Anybody who gives them a convincing story—and dangles some impossibly great result in front of them—they just go ahead with blind trust and hand over a substantial sum of money. That's the Bernie Madoff story in a nutshell.

Many of these elaborate financial scams involve artificial complexities and words meant to intimidate the investor. One word you hear all the time when people are trying to get you to invest is *tranche*, as in, "There will be a tranche of money coming in on this date." This is not a word in common usage; it is a financial term meaning the transfer or movement of a certain sum at a specified time. If I were to lend you $100,000, I would give you four $25,000 tranches every three months. People want to seem smart and knowledgeable. They don't want to admit that they have no idea what a tranche or other "term of art" means.

Here's another great term: default swaps, a term that was in play a lot during all the housing deals, many of them fraudulent. Unless you're in the business, why would you know anything about credit default swaps? Most people don't understand them, do not have a clue. It's another simple concept with a complicated name, and con men use such terms to intimidate people from whom they're trying to extract money.

We live in an age today that is an entirely different world than the one that existed forty years ago. Now, information is available on the computer at the touch of a button, and we're in an international market. Consequently, when banks are lending money at 3 percent, how in the world would you be able to lend somebody money and get a 25 percent return on your investment? At the minimum this is a very high-risk proposition. You don't need a lawyer to tell you this stuff. All you really need is common sense . . . which many people are sadly lacking.

I would say in an average week I look over two different deals clients of mine are considering as investments. I probably approve one to three per year. They're not all scams, but many are. The rest are just promoters with unrealistic expectations, projecting results that are much too good to be true.

Recently a client of mine received a quarter of a million dollars in a settlement. I said to her when she got the check, "What are you going to do with the money?" "Oh, I'm going to invest it," she said. "Great, give me a call when you're ready; I've got some recommendations. We'll toss around some ideas about stocks or investment accounts. Whatever you do," I warned her, "I do not want you going into any partnerships. I do not want you loaning money to anybody for any reason. I don't want you going into your own business; you already have a profession in which you were successful."

"I found the greatest deal!" she announced when she phoned a month later. "25 percent return a year on my investment, guaranteed!"

"You're not doing it," I told her flatly. She started telling me some plans about buying foreclosed houses, rehabbing them, and flipping them. I interrupted her. "Who brought this great deal to you anyway?"

"Oh, the friend of a friend . . . blah blah blah."

"No. Don't even bother showing me the paperwork, because it doesn't make any sense. Why would you take significant money and take that kind of risk when you don't need to? You're just going to trust this friend of a friend? Why would this person pay you 25 percent interest? It's not like you're a real estate expert, running part of the business—you're just a lender." There was more, but you get the idea. Let me put it very simply: You don't get 25 percent in a 3–4 percent world. Remember that, folks.

People get ripped off all the time by their lawyer, their accountant, their real estate broker. Listen. The easiest people to scam are sports figures, music people, actors, doctors, and lawyers. Doctors are the absolute worst, and believe you me, lawyers are right behind them. Your average doctor, a regular internist let's say, knows all about the body, health, and medicine. He or she does not know a damn thing about real estate or finance or anything else, but they think they do. Lawyers also tend to think they're smarter than they really are. All the people I have listed in the above professions have big incomes and usually big egos to match. They are just pigeons waiting to be ripped off!

I get particularly upset when I see elderly people getting taken for their entire life savings. I've got to be honest with you, when a Beverly Hills surgeon who earns a million dollars a year gets taken for a couple hundred thousand dollars, it doesn't personally bother me that much. "It's just money." But a seventy-six-year-old of modest means who loses every penny he had because someone talked him into some "safe" investment? That infuriates me. There are countless people out there who prey on the elderly. They sell names of suckers back and forth!

It's very difficult to recover money from these kinds of scams. You're not going to be able to get your money back if the person who ripped you off no longer has it. Anyone who goes to great lengths to extract big sums of money from you will not have the funds to pay you back if and when they are ever caught. Usually, they've blown it on their own lifestyle, secreted it where no one will ever find it, or are paying off previous investors in whatever Ponzi scheme they're running. By the time you get to the point of locating them and prosecuting them, there's usually very little money to recover.

Scams are not all about complicated investments; I see every kind of rip-off there is out there. I just finished a matter where a female client gave her fiancé $100,000 to invest for her. She'd known him six months. A private investigator could have quickly told her she wasn't getting married . . . because he already had a wife! This is not unusual. What can I tell you?

These guys are out there absolutely preying on women on these dating websites. There's one that claims to do a background check on its members, but believe me, that's nonsense. They don't check anything substantial. There are some real con men out there. And don't get me started on female "escorts." Some of whom have gotten many, many millions of dollars out of poor sap men. Love and lust make complete fools out of so many people. I am not moralizing and believe an adult can do whatever he/she wishes if it doesn't harm others. Just don't mix your money into the relationship.

Then there are those smaller but annoying scams that are cloaked in semi-legitimacy because a famous or quasi-famous person is endorsing them. Joe Blow who used to be a big quarterback is recommending you buy this insurance. This past-his-prime actor is recommending gold coins or silver bars as an investment. I see these kinds of infomercials on TV all the time, and I just shake my head. I know they'll get busted somewhere down the road, just like the others that you've all heard about when it was too late for the people who put money into the scheme. Think for one minute about how much these TV spots cost to produce, and how many suckers are falling for this stuff!

I could go on endlessly, but I hope you've gotten the idea. When I was a young boy, my father told me, "Never play cards with someone using their own deck." Good advice. We must all be cautious of anybody who offers a favor, or the opportunity to make a lot of money. Let me close by recounting what I told my own daughter on the occasion of her twenty-first birthday. When somebody offers to do you a big favor, or to let you in on an opportunity that's too good to be true, always ask yourself, what is their motivation? Why are they doing this? Because there is only one person in this world who truly and unselfishly has your best interests at heart, and that's *me*. Your parent. Everyone else, look out!

Steven A. Silverstein
Silverstein and Huston
Orange, California

6

GREED

Love of Money Is the Root of All Evil

Orange County, California, where I have been in business and lived for three decades, is a wealthy community. Beachside homes in communities like Newport Beach and Crystal Cove are some of the most desirable and expensive real estate in the country. Boats, sports cars, and luxury stores dot the landscape. What has continually astonished me over the years is how foolish so many rich people can be with their money. Wouldn't you think someone with a spare five million dollars to invest might do some homework before handing over so much money? I can't tell you how many people I've met who own a helicopter and live in a ten-million-dollar mansion with its own landing pad . . . but don't have enough sense to come in out of the rain when it comes to investments.

There are five or six billionaires living right here where I'm based, and over the years I've come in contact with several of them. They're always the smartest person in the room—and the unhappiest. Now I am sure there are some happy billionaires, somewhere—perhaps in a different part of America, or Saudi Arabia, or some other distant country. But the men I've met all have serious trouble with their families, kids, ex-spouses; addiction and dysfunction seem to be an occupational hazard in these households. I see happier, more fulfilled men and women every day flipping burgers at beachside food stands. The problem with working for these guys is that they're smart enough to hire the best for advice, but too smart to take it. They've been three steps ahead of everybody else since they were kids. They'll solicit your advice, pay well for it, then ignore it.

But let's talk about your garden-variety multimillionaire, a very common species in Southern California. I get a great deal of business from people who have entrusted their money to a certain advisor, or put it into a certain company, who then call and ask us to investigate. Very rarely do people come to us *before* they transfer the funds, when it would help. It's only when they get the sinking feeling that something is not quite right—and it usually isn't—that they come to us.

We've had countless ballplayers, entertainers, and dot-com millionaires show up and say something like, "I've invested my money in the ABC fund; what do you think about that?" They're looking for us to reassure them with good news, which is not our usual reaction. The vast majority of the time we have the opposite of good news for them. Where they've put their money is in a Ponzi scheme at best. I can generally knock it out with just a question or two.

How much interest are you getting is a great start. Twenty-four percent? Really? I don't even need to take their money for a consultation. I tell them right away, "You are screwed. You need to get your money out, pronto. Before they give it to somebody else." Any investor in this day and age is completely delusional to think anyone can deliver 12 percent return on any investment, much less twenty-four!

Let's consider a middle-of-the-road diverse account, low-risk, from a reputable firm: a 7 percent return is amazing. Eight percent is out of this world. When somebody tells me they've been promised 13 percent, I don't need to see or hear more. Such a return is just not possible. What you should consider before any investment is an extensive background/asset search on a subject or firm, one that will tell you definitively whether or not you should invest with this person or company.

Why do otherwise smart people fall for such pie-in-the-sky numbers? Very simple. They're greedy. One of the smartest clients I ever had was a female doctor with an attorney husband. Both were at the top of their fields; both quite brilliant. And guess to whom they entrusted two million dollars? You got it . . . Bernie Madoff. There were some interesting things about Bernie that made his particular con almost irresistible. One, you had to be personally referred to him—which made people feel as if they were getting in on a secret insider deal.

Secondly, he always started off by demurring . . . *Oh no, I can't accept your money. . . . I can't possibly take on any new clients.* You had to practically beg him to accept your cash. What a great con man that guy was!

A little-known fact: a potential client of Bernie's actually hired a private investigator early on in his investing days. This PI was a novice in the financial arena; he had no special training in investments or accounting and was the first to admit it. His client in New York hired him to check out this supposed investment guru, Bernie Madoff. This guy made his inquiries and three days later concluded, "I've never seen anything close to what this guy is doing. This is the biggest Ponzi scheme imaginable!" He actually took his findings to the state's attorney general and dropped the file into his lap.

Unfortunately, the attorney general dismissed him as some small-town, smalltime PI. He had bigger fish to fry at the time. Flash forward years later: this guy was the very first witness at Madoff's hearing. He was quite forthcoming. He stated right up front that he had very little experience with numbers, but even so had been easily able to see what was going on. Remember, this was no financial whiz. Just a typical investigator. If only more people had done what his client did!

Here's a much more recent example. It happens all the time. As I drank my morning coffee the other day, I read in the *Los Angeles Times* that the Irvine Police Department had arrested three people for their part in an elaborate swindle that defrauded more than a dozen people out of nearly a million dollars. A man named Steven Sears, presenting himself as an attorney specializing in investments, promised people he would preserve and protect their assets by putting them into legitimate corporations. The problem was that all the corporations were fake, owned by Sears himself.

This kind of fraud is easily preventable. Sears used aliases. For a mere twenty-dollar fee, a surname index check by a local PI would have revealed his numerous aliases, multiple dates of birth, and several Social Security numbers—raising a huge red flag to any potential investor. Also, a free check on the Internet would have revealed that he was disbarred as an attorney in 2011. All you have to do is google "State Bar of ___," entering your state's name. This will take you to the state's bar website, where clicking "attorney search" will give you all the information you ever wanted: current status, bar number, e-mail, phone and fax numbers, address, any disciplinary actions, and more.

This kind of work is well within the purview of any solid investigator. Any competent PI should be able to give you a very good idea of exactly who you are doing business with for less than a thousand dollars. They go through a proprietary database called the United States Consumer Public Filing Index, which handles five things: bankruptcies, notice of defaults, judgments, tax liens, and problems with the IRS. Obviously, these are all issues that should be checked out. Most people simply aren't aware of it or know how to hire someone to access this data.

Among other things, this index will tell you if a person had their house foreclosed on, owes money to the IRS, or has any judgments against them. Let's say we check out an investment firm in St. Louis and discover they have thirty-five pending civil cases against them. Would you still want to invest? Not only can a good PI tell you where not to put your money, we can tell you where you should invest your money. At my firm, we have set categories for every level of investor: zero to $500,000; $500,000 to a million; one to ten million; and above ten million. We recommend different advisors and plans for each; there's no "one size fits all." Different rules and strategies come into play depending on the amount and your tolerance for risk.

Let me stress that this information applies to everybody making investments, not just millionaires. Anyone looking to invest any amount of money would do themselves a tremendous favor by hiring a good PI to help them with this decision. Most people work hard for their money. It's always a surprise to me how frequently average people work against themselves. I hope I have encouraged you to do your homework. Don't be the next person to read about their "financial advisor" in the paper!

❊ ❊ ❊

Many of the multimillionaires I deal with are entrepreneurs who spent a good portion of their lives and plenty of sweat equity building a successful business. It used to be standard that 15 percent of the employees in any given company of fifty or more employees were stealing time, money, or product. That number remained consistent for decades throughout corporate America. In 2008, when the economic meltdown and housing crisis hit and the entire bubble burst, that number rose sharply and immediately.

The reason why is simple: no more Christmas bonus, no more holiday parties, no more free lunches, no more raises—and to add insult to injury, being frequently told, "You're lucky to have work at all," in a dismal job market. Employees became resentful and started to think, "I'm going to get mine, somehow." Believe me, they did . . . by stealing. In the investigative community, we all started calling each other and asking, "Have you noticed an increase in this kind of activity?" None of us could believe what we were seeing. From that time until the present day, more than a decade later, the new figure has stayed steady: in any given company of fifty or more employees, a staggering 75 *percent* of the workforce is stealing time, money, or product.

It used to require great skill to find out who stole the company golf cart, for example. Now employees are truly brazen. In the eighties and nineties people would say things like, "You got me," and sigh, and sometimes cry. They'd at least act a little remorseful. These days? I sit across from men and women who don't display the slightest concern or regret that they've been caught red-handed. "Yeah I took it, so what? It's been five years since I got a raise or a bonus, I only get a week of vacation a year . . . He's not even going to miss ten grand!" They have what is to me a breathtaking sense of entitlement, a "so what are you gonna do to me" attitude. I see this attitude across the board in terms of age . . . it's not just the younger "millennial" generation; oftentimes, it's older, long-term employees who are the most embittered.

Back in the early eighties, I was just getting my business going. I was no longer a sole proprietor; I had one investigator and a small office in a shopping center. A jewelry store, a bridal boutique, and a woman's dress store were our neighbors. It was a great area for my female-centric business; all those women coming to shop were intrigued by my sign, Martin Investigative Services; they'd poke their heads in to see what we were all about.

I became friendly with the jewelry store owner, who complained to me one day, "Lately I'm losing my ass! I can't for the life of me figure out what's going on! I'd hire you, but I can't afford your services." Back at that time, I was charging the grand sum of thirty or thirty-five dollars an hour. I wanted to be a good neighbor, so I offered to investigate as a courtesy. I thought maybe we could take it out in trade later.

I went to his shop and interviewed his six employees. Afterward, as we met in my office, I said, "I've got to tell you. These are the best six employees I've ever seen. I used all my interrogation and interview skills and found nothing. There is no way any of those people are stealing from you; I can only conclude that you're a terrible businessman."

"No, it's something else." He shook his head. "Paul and I just cannot figure out what is going on . . . "

"Paul?" I said. "Wait a minute, who's Paul?"

"Paul's my guy in the back. He is the actual designer and maker of our jewelry."

"Well, why didn't I interview him?"

"There's no need; he's the artist. . . . Besides, he's been with me for years. Decades. There's no way."

I went to see Paul, nonetheless. I sat down in his cramped dark space, hidden away behind the showroom, and said, "We need to have a little chat, Paul. I've been doing this a long time and I know something is very wrong. I also imagine you do not want me to take my suspicions over to the DA's office, so it's best you come clean. Right now. I need to know how much you stole. Let's start with last night."

He spilled it, immediately. The words came tumbling out. In a nutshell, he had started stealing loose stones, mostly diamonds, and selling them on the side. The reason? He had suddenly realized that after working at the jewelry store for thirty-seven years, he had no retirement plan. So he decided to fund his own. The store owner was heartbroken. He had been betrayed by his best friend of decades—a possibility he had never even imagined.

I asked other private investigators, "So, what do you do when you catch somebody stealing from your clients?" Most of them shrugged and said something along the lines of, "I dunno . . . we tell the owner to get rid of 'em!" I was surprised. I was coming from a law enforcement background where we did everything in our power to prosecute major drug dealers. I was in a kick-ass-take-names mode, but nobody else was. I wanted to see justice done! I was in for a bit of a wake-up call.

✵ ✵ ✵

In what was one of the biggest fraud cases my company ever handled, a man in Orange County who was the accountant for a transportation company was suspected of stealing huge sums from his employer through a complex system of fake invoicing. Three of us went in to grill him—myself and two of my best investigators. We entered the conference room and sat down to have a very serious conversation with this guy, ready to use all our best interrogative techniques. We were hoping just to get him to cop to something small, to get the ball rolling. Not two minutes into it the guy held up his hands. "I did it. I know exactly how much I took . . . nearly two million dollars . . . one-point-eight to be exact."

"So what did you do with it?"

"Bet on the Lakers. Bought a boatload of cocaine. And partied with some really hot hookers down in Costa Rica." Well, that was a fast investigation. We gathered all the supporting background materials—copies of the phony checks, dummy invoices, and phone records. I sorted it, organized it, wrapped it all up, and basically tied a red bow around it before heading off to a local police department in Orange County.

"Yeah . . . not sure we're going to get involved in this," was what I heard when I followed up a couple weeks later.

"Are you kidding me?! This is not pocket change. It's nearly two million dollars!" I protested. For two months, I pestered them. I wasn't about to let this go down without a fight. "You don't have to do any work," I pointed out. "We've laid it all out for you. Just present this to the district attorney, file charges, have him arrested, and take the case to court . . . he's already admitted he's guilty! There's a signed declaration of guilt right on top!"

Finally, I wore them down. A detective did take the file to the DA's office, where one of their investigators reviewed the material. The DA's office did file charges, and the guy was arrested. When it came time for the trial, he pleaded "not guilty." His reason for that was, "Those guys said if I told them the truth, they'd let me out of this." Our jaws dropped. If only we had that kind of power. The trial proceeded, with the question basically now becoming, "So were you lying then to these investigators, or are you lying now?" Eventually, after an eighteen-month legal process, uphill every step of the way, he was sentenced to five years.

It became clear to me that criminals are rarely prosecuted for business crimes such as embezzlement the way the general public might imagine. Law enforcement is up to their eyeballs in work. Many police forces no longer pay overtime, which quickly becomes a problem. For every one case that comes in the door, there are ten more just as urgent right behind them. Don't forget that police officers are used to seeing the worst of human nature. Sometimes, they can have what appears to be a pretty cavalier reaction to your misfortune.

What they see is that you founded and built up a business. You hired, supervised, and trusted a bookkeeper, let's say, who embezzled tens of thousands of dollars over a few years from you, a considerable sum for any small business. This happens all the time, every day. They see that this misfortune was enough to drive your business under. Again, nothing new here; it happens all the time. Unfortunately, their reaction tends to be, "If you're dumb enough to actually have somebody steal that kind of money from you, maybe you deserve it." Let me be real here. Even when I go in and tell an officer, "This person stole a million dollars from my client!" their reaction is likely to be . . . blank stare. Yawn. "So . . . what did you think of the game last night?"

Even if you manage to get the thieves arrested, you will often come up against a bleeding-heart prosecutor who, weighing the time and costs of going to trial, says, "It really wasn't *that* much." On the flip side, you get a super-tough prosecutor who says, "Look. I've got six murder cases, four rape cases, and an armed robbery on my plate. Frankly, I really don't care about your case. What, your client didn't notice forty thousand dollars missing? Which is he—stupid or asleep?"

Good question! So where are the owners when this stuff happens? In the last major case my company handled—an engineering firm with numerous city contracts whose senior managers were stealing the owner blind with all kinds of sophisticated scams—the owner was in Hawaii. He needed a vacation. When I called to tell him there was some very serious stuff going on in terms of fraud, his response was, "Handle it." He hates confrontation, which I have found is a very typical trait in upper-echelon corporate America.

It's also a dangerous human trait, the same one that causes people to simply watch as their investments melt away when the economy crumbles and the stock market crashes. So many refuse to get out until it's too late. They stay and stay and stay. This particular client let a gang of pirates into the company he spent decades building and hoped to leave to his children. He then buried his head in the sand as his life's work was literally dismantled all around him. I will give this particular owner some credit: he had an attorney who was smart enough to call us in to stop the bleeding. Had another thirty days gone by, the company would have folded. As it stood, we got a chance to save it.

Many of these multimillionaire entrepreneurs have on blinders. They don't want to see reality. They think they're really good managers when they are not. It's a matter of ego, sometimes. These guys have built very successful companies; things have gone along fine so far . . . they simply can't accept that they've been had or outsmarted. Also, rightly or wrongly, a surprising number of them are invested in believing that they're good guys, fair bosses, well-liked and respected by their employees. They just don't want to believe that anyone would want to steal from them.

To that, I can only shake my head.

✶ ✶ ✶

How much more successful could all these entrepreneurs and their companies I've mentioned have been had they stayed vigilant and monitored things more carefully? It's not easy to sit across the table from a CEO who earns $11 million a year and tell him that he doesn't have all the answers. They think they're cooking with all five engines because their company grosses $100 million a year? My hat's off to you. You are a very accomplished human being. But you could be making $200 million!

This is the real bottom line: You have got to stay on top of your employees. They will test you all the time. When—not if, *when*—they take an inch and nothing happens, they'll take another inch. When nothing happens again, they'll take six inches . . . then a foot, then a yard, then they're really off to the races. The most important lesson any business owner or entrepreneur can take to heart is: Trust Nobody. Never fall asleep at the switch. Everybody's guilty until proven innocent, no matter how long they've been with you. Sound harsh? It's a tough world out there.

If you are an entrepreneur or HR person or work as a senior manager, I can't recommend strongly enough that you undergo a security risk analysis of your business every six months. You have probably never thought about having a PI come in and just talk to your people. It is not going to cost you much to have a first-class private investigator come in and review your personnel and operations; I would estimate the cost to be $5,000. What if they save you $100,000? Isn't that money well spent? I have never yet conducted a security review at a business where we did not save the client money (see http://www.taskforceconsulting.com).

When it comes to this kind of job, I don't believe in undercover work. Some private investigators like to send an undercover person into the manufacturing plant or office to set up an elaborate sting. They do this whether they're charged with finding out who's drinking, who's stealing from the warehouse, or who's banging the girls in the back room. I don't find that kind of lengthy, expensive surveillance necessary. Our interview skills have been honed to the point we can get an employee to cop to whatever's going on by interrogating them in a conference room. Once someone admits to guilt, it all starts to spill out, including taking down the rest of the rats on the ship.

Product and money are both tangible; easy to see when it's gone missing. Business owners might say, "I'm not missing any product. I'm not missing any money; therefore, I'm doing fine." Really? Are you sure? Time is always less of a concern. People say, "ahhhhh, no big deal." Sure, we might be talking about a secretary taking a half-hour extra for lunch. But how about the old clocking in for other employees so that a three-hour break is punched in and out as a thirty-minute lunch? How about the employee who spends six of his eight hours at work playing solitaire on his computer? Believe me, I just spoke to a $140,000-per-year supervisor last week who did just that all day, every day. "Oh sure, yeah, sometimes I play on my computer . . . everyone does," was his response. Are you going to tell me that is not flat-out stealing from his employer?

Or yet another employee who was confronted with having filled his wife's car up with gas on the company card. "What's the big deal?" he asked in all seriousness. He was actually acting annoyed I would even bring this up. Really? Last time I filled my tank it cost fifty dollars. What if every employee did this? This kind of petty chiseling adds up to a staggering amount of money if you have fifty employees. If each one of your fifty employees who makes $20 an hour steals just one hour a week, that's $1000 a week. Fifty-two thousand dollars a year out the door. That's a significant amount of money for a smaller business.

The real issue, as I said, is that once they start stealing time, they quickly move on to more tangible rewards: money and/or product. Getting away with things only emboldens people. Facing zero consequences for stealing time, I can assure business owners that such activity will soon progress. The idea is to stay on top of these matters from the start, so you don't call us too late.

Just last month an energy drink company I investigated folded because the accounting person was embezzling and the warehouse guys were stealing pallets of product and selling it at swap meets every weekend. Now this owner's wiped out, missing money and his product, and screaming bloody murder, saying, "Why can't the cops do something about this?" I am happy to go visit the cops. But I know how these matters frequently turn out. Not to sound jaded, but I have seen too many people skate.

I also recently got a call from a finance company here in Southern California. This company has done very well for themselves; they were very careful about where they lent money. Their return on investment rate is high; they have carefully cultivated their blue-chip client base. Recently the owners were approached by a group who wanted to invest big money into their company. And for the very first time in my career, I was asked to check out people who wanted to write them a million-dollar check.

The smartass part of me, of course, says, if anyone wants to hand you a million dollars, why ask questions? Because they're really smart. They want to make sure this money is clean—not drug money, not being laundered—from a legitimate group of people with solid business reputations. How did these people make their money? Do they have tax problems? Judgments? Bankruptcies? Ties to criminals? That's what I'm being paid to find out. Now these new clients of mine are a bit paranoid, but brilliant. They are going to go far!

* * *

I truly thought at this stage of my life I could no longer be shocked by anyone's greed. Then my actuary, who advised me on how to build up my retirement fund, came to call. We'd worked together for twenty-some years; he was one of the most honest guys I ever met. Unbelievably sharp, with a great client list. Six months ago, he walked into my office and said, "I've got a problem, I need to talk to you."

"Sure, what is it?"

"I just pleaded guilty to twelve counts in the state of New York."

"*What?* What did you do?"

"I took people's money," he said. "And didn't give it back, basically. It was pretty much a big Ponzi scheme."

I was stunned. "Are you kidding me, you have more clients than you know what to do with! You're a wealthy guy already!" He was, for sure, in the top 1 or 2 percent of earners. "You've got houses, cars, great educations for your kids . . . what the hell were you thinking?" He didn't have an answer.

He was hoping I could help him become a government informant, to work some time off so he wouldn't have to go to prison. That didn't happen because he didn't have anything to offer to the government. He didn't know any bad guys; he was just a numbers guy who got greedy! He got sentenced to thirteen years. This was the last guy in the history of mankind I would have predicted would, or could, go bad. It jolted me into remembering the lessons I learned long ago.

Studying in a seminary really brought home to me the fact that everything we own will be owned by someone else, someday. All the material possessions we prize so highly are only ours for a very short time. We would all do well to keep that in mind!

Chris Copps is a founding partner of Corient Capital Partners, one of the largest, privately owned, independent wealth management firms in the nation, headquartered in beautiful Newport Beach, California. Corient focuses exclusively on serving a select number of ultra-affluent individuals, their families, and their companies. The team consists of seven partners, one managing director, two analysts, and five support staff.

Corient was founded in 2015; however, the partners all worked together previously at Merrill Lynch. Each partner has an average of eighteen years in the industry, adding up to over a hundred years of aggregate experience; Chris personally has been in this business for three decades. All the partners put in time at the big firms. Chris did stints at Kidder Peabody, J. P. Morgan, and Hambrecht and Quist. With what's happening at the larger financial institutions, it's become increasingly more painful to work there. Senior management is primarily focused on the amount of revenue each advisor can generate for the firm.

Corient came to the conclusion that life was too short to work with people they didn't like or respect—both from a partner perspective and a client perspective. The most important thing for all of them is trust, honesty, and respect for each other and the clients they serve. They wanted a more family-like atmosphere, which is diametrically opposed to the way big banks run. They have the big firm experience and background, just not the attitude.

The stated minimum account size at Corient is ten million dollars; the average account size is between twenty to thirty million. So they're working with an ultra-affluent group of clients. Still, even this sophisticated group of investors is not immune to having been taken for a ride by unscrupulous advisors, or from making the same mistakes more average-income people do. Whether they committed their money to an investment idea that was too good to be true, took a "surefire" tip from their brother-in-law, or didn't vet their advisor carefully enough, they make the same mistakes—just on a larger scale.

The integrity of Corient's financial advisors must be above reproach. Their personal values are at the core of how they operate their business. They also run a very tight ship in terms of openness and transparency. There are many money managers and investment advisors out there who take control of the money, make the investment decisions, and also report on the results. That was a significant issue with the Madoff investment scheme . . . there were virtually no checks and balances in place. With Corient, clients' money is actually held at a third-party custodian (i.e., Fidelity, Schwab, or Bank of New York).

As far as knowing exactly where the money is at all times, and its safety and security, Corient clients get a separate statement from Fidelity (or whoever the institution may be). They are also provided a Corient statement every month, which can easily be checked against their custody statements to make sure they reconcile.

Being an independent firm, the safety and security of clients' assets rank first and foremost. The partners at Corient are as concerned with risk management and legacy planning as they are with generating impressive investment returns. Most clients come to Corient already rich. A partner's job is to keep them that way and not take unnecessary risks. A Corient client's core portfolio is typically quite conservative, though the company does have a very interesting professional network, offering unique access to high-quality alternative investment opportunities, which adds considerable value for their customers.

Personal and cyber security is also very important, especially for wealthy families who travel abroad frequently, whether is personal safety, home security, or traveling safely. Security is an important watchword at Corient—another key issue they take very seriously. They have a great network of high-quality, fully vetted experts they can count on to satisfy these security needs.

People make the same investment mistakes across all income levels, and the main problem advisors see over and over is succumbing to emotions. When things are going great, momentum is positive, and the stock market or real estate markets are booming, that's usually when people want to get in. When all is lost and doom and gloom, that's when they want to get out. Most individual investors make the wrong investments at the wrong times due to their emotions. Corient spends a great deal of time playing financial psychologist to their clients.

The individual investor actually makes about half the return on the market for that very reason: making the wrong decision at the wrong time due to emotional factors. In fact, this is also true mainly for the more "average" middle-class investor. The more sophisticated investor generally has advisors or they've done it before and know that long-term, thoughtful, strategic planning is best.

Corient has chosen to work on a very high end of the scale, but given those odds, they encourage everyone to seek out a qualified financial advisor. There are plenty of fine people out there who work with smaller investors and know just what to do with grandma's IRA. This is actually a much harder job, because when clients have less money, it's generally more important to them. Volatility in the markets causes much more distress to the smaller investor. If you have a couple million in your retirement account and the market goes down 10 to 20 percent, that's a significant hit. If you have twenty million and the same thing happens, you're generally more able to cope.

It's important to Chris and his partners to come to the office each day and work with colleagues they truly like, trust, and respect. They love to spar and encourage vigorous discussion and differences of opinions, but they do not tolerate abusive behavior. The industry often encourages and rewards mean-spiritedness, greed, and winning at all costs. They were once in that environment. They know how the other side lives.

Chris mentioned that he has fired clients before—that's one of his less pleasant duties as a founding partner. Mainly, it's for reasons of personality. Corient won't tolerate abusive behavior. If the clients are not good, quality, ethical people, the company is not interested in working with them, no matter how large their portfolio is. Life is too short to have to have to endure people you don't respect.

Chris claims that Corient is successful because of their clients. When you step into their spectacular ocean-view offices in Fashion Island, you can feel the difference. They truly consider themselves one big family. Corient has brought many people together for quality friendships and unique investment opportunities. This is the kind of service you should look for, no matter what size investor you are.

7

DISAPPEARED

In the three decades since I founded my agency, official reports on missing persons have increased sixfold. When adults "disappear," there are generally three possibilities: foul play, suicide, or the person has chosen to walk away from his or her own life. Here is what you need to know right off the bat: Law enforcement does not have the time or resources to handle 90 percent of the missing persons cases that are officially reported. That's not an exact statistic, of course, but after handling hundreds of these cases, I feel pretty confident in that number. Any "disappearance" is another instance where the right private investigator can be your best friend.

Consider a large metropolitan police department like the Los Angeles Police Department, with its huge adult missing persons department. Their detectives never close a case until the person is found. These guys are good, some of the best investigators in the country. But they are absolutely buried under the crush of cases. How many cases do you think they handle? Well, they get 10–15 new missing persons *a day* reported to them.

I want to make you aware of this reality, because should an adult in your life vanish, you are pretty much on your own. I stress that this is not because law enforcement personnel are heartless or unwilling to work hard . . . just stretched too thin. Officers taking the initial report on a missing person aged eighteen or older tend to do the bare minimum. That is, fill out a report, thank you for coming in, and tell you that the odds are the missing person will likely get in touch soon. Then it's good-bye and good luck.

Here is the best advice I can give anyone going to the station to give a missing persons report: Do not get an incident report number; insist on a police report number. An incident report is simply a receipt given to anybody who reports anything at all. You go to the station, pour out your heart, show photos, and ask for help. You leave clutching a copy of an incident report in your hand, thinking you've done all you can. But that receipt? Originals are generally forwarded to a dead file and rarely, if ever, seen again. A case number will actually be forwarded to a detective. Next, I would advise you to retain your own private investigator.

Martin Investigative Services handles disappearances differently from most other agencies. We are serious about solving the case quickly, and have no intention of stringing clients along, which sadly can happen when hiring the wrong PI. Some PIs wait to gauge the emotional stability of the client in such a stressful situation and use that as their barometer of what to charge—highly unethical. An open-ended budget with no controls is something consumers must watch out for.

For me, in order for me to be able to do anything for you, I will require two things. My first question to a client is: Do you have a police report? I'll need to review it. Secondly, there must be sufficient reason for me to believe I have a chance of finding this person to take the case. I need to be able to find a hook, something I can exploit to locate this person. I want to be able to return to the police, have them dig that report out of an overflowing in-basket, and move it to the top of the pile.

Law enforcement and I will work as a team, because there are things I can do that cops can't, and things cops can do that I can't. When I come on board, I go over and tell the police that I've been retained and ask if they mind if I do everything in my power to conduct my own investigation. They will almost invariably say go ahead, we don't have the manpower to give this as much time as you can, and give me carte blanche to do whatever I can to help.

I then sit down with the family and come up with an angle to play up in the press. What makes this case different or more unusual or compelling than any of the other hundreds of missing persons cases that happen all the time in Southern California? I want publicity, and I want lots of it. I want to call a press conference and get this person's face all over the newspapers, television, and Internet. Reporters are a jaded bunch. If they don't hear something to capture their interest, they'll just leave—or even worse, not show up in the first place. I need to grab their attention and get them invested. I want them to want to solve this mystery along with me. I need them on my side to get the public involved.

I start to get nervous if we haven't resolved a missing persons case in seventy-two hours, or at least have a very solid lead on the subject, because most cases are clearly solvable within that time frame. Of course, we will continue to work the case until the person is found or every last lead is exhausted, but there are those that, despite heroic efforts on everybody's part, are never resolved. The kind of cases that keep me up at night. The kind of case that breaks everybody's heart.

* * *

In the summer of 2014, twenty-six-year-old Derek Adam Seehausen, one of the top medical students in the country, was in his last semester of medical school at the University of Southern California. He was bright and athletic, blessed with a loving family and many close friends. Police would determine that the last official sighting of him was at an ATM in the Echo Park neighborhood where he rented an apartment. Casually dressed in plaid shorts and a hoodie, he was filmed withdrawing two hundred dollars cash at approximately 10:35 p.m. He walked out of the frame and simply vanished into the bustle of Alvarado Street.

His friends quickly raised the alarm when the conscientious student did not appear for classes, and an official report was filed. The police did a great job tracking his last known movements; when the family reached out to me, I didn't think there was more I could do to help them and reluctantly told them so. Then, about ten days after he disappeared, there was a sighting of a man who appeared to be Derek riding on a Los Angeles Metro bus. I decided to use the latest sighting, complete with surveillance photographs, as my hook. I took the case, called a press conference at the USC campus, and jumped into the investigation, certain we would soon locate this young man. As his devastated mother said, "If you took 1,000 people, Derek would be last in line to do this."

My team and I turned Derek's life inside out. We interviewed dozens of classmates, professors, friends, family members, and neighbors. We sorted out all the various conflicting stories and rumors floating around. There were some ambiguities in the case, as there are in any disappearance, and it's the investigator's job to sort the wheat from the chaff. It was initially reported that Derek had been suicidal; that assertion was later corrected after his family and friends vehemently denied it. It was true that he had paid a friend back for a loan the night he vanished. It was also true that he had recently suffered a setback in his studies, and a vaguely worded note was found on his computer. However, he'd also made plans for the weekend with a friend and was excited about his upcoming graduation, which he discussed with his mother just a day or two before he went missing.

Here's what I know for sure after thousands of missing persons investigations: You can kill yourself, sure, but you can't bury yourself . . . so where are the bodies of these people who vanish? In the case of suicide, that's what we are hired to find out. One problem with suicides: when a person jumps off a twenty-fifth floor balcony, or is pulled from underwater after a few weeks of being submerged, their body no longer looks at all as it did during life. We stayed on top of every hospital, morgue, and crime report in the area and were able to rule out foul play and any John Does.

Most people who kill themselves want their bodies to be found. It's a bit like that famous old epitaph you see on tombstones: "I told you I was sick." Some just want people to know they weren't bluffing. Mainly, most people who commit suicide are fundamentally decent. They do not want their families to suffer by never knowing what happened to them. They might kill themselves, but they don't go out to the middle of the ocean, slit their wrists, and drop to the bottom of the sea, never to be found. That sentences friends and family to years and years of purgatory. After all I learned about Derek in our intensive investigation, I concluded he was just too nice a kid to do this to the many people who loved him.

We did a first-class thorough investigation into his disappearance and came up empty-handed. Several years later, my belief is that Derek was temporarily overwhelmed by some academic pressures, made a rash decision to vanish, and is now too embarrassed to come back. For all I know, he's working in a hospital today down in Mexico. At least, I hope that's the case. I still hope I'll find him. As usual, this year I will do some follow-up work on his case. I'll reach out online and in the press on Derek's birthday and the anniversary of his disappearance and urge him to contact me or his family. I will continue to do so every year for the rest of my life, as I do for others I simply have not found.

* * *

One of the reasons I feel Derek may still be alive and well is because he was exceptionally bright and resourceful. Most people simply do not have the discipline to walk away from their old life and start a new one. It's hard work to maintain a brand-new identity, what with the change in name, Social Security number, occupation, and lifestyle it requires. As a former federal agent, I knew several informants who we put into the witness protection program. And I am here today, as a private investigator, to say that even someone in the witness protection program can be found. The fastest and easiest way is to have law enforcement monitor the missing person's mother's phone calls and/or package deliveries on Mother's Day and her birthday. Even the worst informers, crooks, and weasels usually still call their mother on those dates!

Add that to the incredibly sophisticated databases in this country and the proliferation of social media over the past decade. As I discussed in the previous chapter, there are all kinds of databases PIs can subscribe to in addition to the considerable amount of information that's out there in the public record, freely accessible to all. These days, it is also impossible for most people to resist communicating on Facebook or Instagram, no matter what their circumstances. The bottom line is that if you live in mainstream America, even just a little bit, we can and will find you. Out of a hundred people we search for, we find 98.8 percent of them. The other 1.2 percent are living completely off the grid—under a rock in Maui or on somebody's couch.

When I left the Department of Justice, it was in the early days of information technology. I couldn't take information with me, of course, so I started keeping my own data, on floppy discs that you inserted in a slot in the computer hard drive. Starting out, I used to buy court and civil records from Orange and Los Angeles Counties. Eventually, we developed our own system, and now Martin Investigative has its own powerful proprietary databases. By running all the information we have through our system, we're bound to turn up *something*.

Even if we just have a scrap, that's usually enough, because there are just so many ways to track a person: name, date of birth, last known address, Social Security number, names of relatives, e-mail addresses, cell phone numbers. By the time a person turns eighteen years of age, we begin collecting data on them. They're in the system. Sometimes people call me up and say, "I'll pay you five thousand dollars to scrub me from the system." I laugh and tell them that they could pay me five million dollars, but I still couldn't wipe anyone out of the system. It's impossible. And that's just public records . . . we're not even getting into what the Feds know. Listen, if they can track down El Chapo, they can certainly find you!

✿ ✿ ✿

Southern California, where I am based, is an absolute mecca for runaway teens. When it comes to runaways, here are some important time frames for parents to consider. Every case must be taken on an individual basis, but I like to get cases within seventy-two hours of the kid's disappearance. It is best to get started right away, but I hate to have parents show up, out of their minds with worry, relate the story, hand over the retainer, and then the kid shows up the next day. Seventy-two hours is generally the "magic number."

Another key number is what I call the ten-day rule for teenage runaways. Anyone who has run away and manages to stay under the radar for ten days becomes much harder to find. The kids learn to blend in, adapt to life off the grid, and become part of the runaway/homeless/ transient population who hide in plain sight on street corners or parks or in squats all over America. After ten days, they have gotten street-savvy. So, if you are looking to retain an investigator, remember that after ten days it becomes much more difficult, time-consuming, and expensive for the person or agency to do their job. If the teen has been gone for longer than two months, the locate process becomes very difficult. By that time, it's a cold trail, an almost impossible task.

One final important number: the thirty-day rule. As I explained earlier, Martin Investigative works for a flat rate. When we take a case, we work the case hard for thirty days; we are strongly motivated to get results fast. After thirty days of hard work with no solid leads to show for it, we start to get very nervous.

When somebody sits down in front of me asking me to find their child, it's a huge responsibility. You usually only get one shot. In our office, we only take one out of ten cases from those who reach out to us. Most of the time, parents call me looking for help, and the kid returns within twenty-four hours. Every single time, I am happy to hear it. Fortunately, the majority of runaways do come home. But for those who don't come back? It's time for us—the professionals—to step in.

Teens rarely run away suddenly, out of the blue. There are numerous signs along the way of trouble that sometimes parents choose to minimize or ignore, hoping it's just a stage. Here are some of the most common signs to watch out for:

- Routine use of alcohol or drugs becomes disruptive, creating problems at school or home
- Quick and major changes in personality
- Lack of interest in school activities or falling grades
- Continuous sadness, depression, persistent anxiety, or lashing out in anger
- Talk or even threats of suicide—a major warning sign that must be taken seriously and addressed
- Rejection of previous friends and sources of support
- Run-ins with the law enforcement community
- Radical changes in appearance, self-mutilation or cutting, or extreme gain or loss of weight
- Defiance: the outright refusal to obey the most basic and reasonable household rules and regulations

Early intervention is ideal, but once they're gone, we jump in wholeheartedly to locate them. Once we decide to take the case, and we figure out our "hook" and take the retainer, we do an extensive interview with the family. We look for a triggering factor: what happened that could have made the person run away? Was there an argument? Punishment? Trouble at school? Breakup with boyfriend or girlfriend? Did the teen take their phone? Are there clothes missing from the closet? Has a friend gone missing as well?

Once we establish these basics, we then ask for a list of the teen's friends, along with addresses and telephone numbers. This is critical, because frequently we can turn the teen up at one of these houses, where another parent is unwittingly breaking the law. Many kind people are simply misled. A friend of their kid comes to them with a sad tale of, "My parents hate me . . . " or "My father beats me . . . " and the concerned parent immediately says, "Oh, please, come and stay with us. We don't want you to be hurt." Or their own teen just says, "Kimmy is going to stay for a couple weeks while her parents are on a cruise," and distracted parents let it slide. In any case, many times they are not getting the full story. Even if the story of abuse is true, the teen is still a minor; it is against the law to take runaway teens in and away from their parents.

Harboring a runaway is an extremely serious matter. I tell every single person I speak to in the course of the investigation, particularly friends of teens, that I am going to find this missing kid. When I find him, and learn that you helped hide him or knew of his whereabouts, I will make every effort to have law enforcement come after you. I make it very clear that it's in everyone's best interest to give up any information now, not later, when it's too late. Forget your misguided loyalty or fear of "snitching." You'd better believe I will do my damnedest to prosecute anyone who hindered an investigation, no matter what their reason.

OK, so you're convinced that the teen has really run and isn't hiding with a friend or relative. It's time to spring into action. Remember what I said earlier about the right private eye being your best friend? The key word is "right." Sadly, there are PIs out there willing to take advantage of desperate families. This kind of PI will just take the retainer, sit back, and pray, basically, that the teen will reappear. Please, take this checklist straight to whatever PI you are considering hiring should you need one. This is what you need to ask:

- *Do you have experience locating missing persons/runaways?* This should go without saying. Ask who they have found and under what circumstances.
- *Are you going to set up a website?* This is absolutely key . . . a website with all the pertinent information must be set up at once

(helpfindmichael.com, for example.) This is the place to monitor tips and make updates.

- *Are you going to bombard social media?* Every update to the site and case should be tweeted, Instagrammed, and Facebooked to all the family's contacts.
- *Will you distribute flyers?* Good old-fashioned flyers are still highly effective. Posted at the school, restaurants, and malls where the kid was known to frequent and the like.
- *Should we offer a reward?* A reward is very necessary; it will highly motivate people to search, help, or tell anything they know. Never offer less than $10,000.
- *Where do you plan to look; and do you have local informants there?* Martin Investigative Services has informants on the streets of every major city: train conductors, bus drivers, employees at homeless shelters, outreach workers, food bank volunteers. Make sure your PI has a network to tap.
- *What is your relationship with local police?* Ideally, the investigator and law enforcement work hand in hand to bring the teenager home.
- *Will you check all local hospitals and morgues?* Checking hospitals is something that can be done by family and friends, but it helps to have a professional overseeing John Does.
- *Are you going to call a press conference?* Do you know how to call a press conference? Do you have contacts with any local or national media? What is the hook you will share to stir up interest in this particular case?
- *Are you skilled in the art of interview and interrogation?* Does your investigator have the demeanor to be able to draw out teenagers and their parents, teachers, coaches? Is he able to communicate to them that this kid is going to die unless they are found and helped?

* * *

As every parent knows, teenage years are a time to rebel, even when the life they are leading looks great on the outside. I have handled every kind of case imaginable over the years. I've talked to runaway teens who told me, "I really enjoyed running away; it was fun. I was doing whatever drugs I wanted, hanging out, having sex . . . " for a rebellious, street-smart kid who is disaffected and doesn't want to go to school, roughing it may seem like a fun lifestyle, at least for a while.

I remember a lovely girl from Florida who I found hanging out with a bunch of other runaway teens in Long Beach. Her angelic face hid a wild streak. She was polite and well-spoken, as we talked for two and a half hours. She told me straight up that she liked to smoke pot, lots of it, and take Adderall recreationally . . . lots of it. "I'm smart," she told me. "I don't have any problems on the street. I'm having a good time. I've got money, I'm fine." Anyway . . . a week or so later she got beat up, badly, and called me from her cheap Anaheim motel room with a change of heart. "OK," she said, "I'm ready to come home." She wasn't quite as tough as she thought she was.

Other kids come from great, privileged homes, but feel too much pressure to achieve, whether that's academically or athletically or getting into the right college. That was the case for a young man I located who was captain of the football team and headed to USC on a water polo scholarship. He felt a tremendous amount of self-imposed pressure and simply snapped. I found him smoking pot on a farm in Oregon.

Naturally, I have encountered plenty of nightmare parents along the way. I had a case last year with sisters who ran away together; I eventually located them more than a thousand miles away in the Midwest. Their father, by his own admission, was a complete horse's ass. Not that he had ever actually abused them, but he was entirely too hard on his girls. Nothing they ever did was good enough. A grade of "B" was unthinkable. He was extremely exacting and demanding and stayed on them mercilessly about everything from their boyfriends to how they dressed to their friends . . . they could not take it anymore.

Then there was the affluent dad who, when I called to say I'd located his missing teenage son, said, "Oh man, I just got a tee time I've been waiting two days to get . . . call me tomorrow" . . . click. Or the mother, upon hearing that I'd located her daughter, and being cautioned that she was not in the best shape physically or emotionally, said to me, "Oh, I'm at the Nordstrom half-yearly sale. I'll get back with you soon." No wonder these kids ran away. In fact, I have to salute many of these kids for making it as long as they have with parents like they have. Southern California is an interesting segment of society, to say the least.

When I take on a runaway child case, I always ask the parent, "What are you going to do when I bring him or her back?" I always encourage the families to be welcoming. Often the kid is afraid to return, or their pride prevents them from making the call. After the reunion, there needs to be behavioral modification on everybody's part. In the eighties, a period when "tough love" was a popular concept, I saw plenty of kids dumped into "boot camps" in the wilderness to survive, or "scared straight" in a military-like program for thirty days to break their spirit, like they were a wild horse. It definitely broke their spirits, but the changes were not long-lasting and caused more permanent damage than lasting, positive change.

I am a big fan of rehab programs, when appropriate, individual and family counseling, fresh starts, and more accountability on everyone's behalf. Over the years, I've come across some fine schools that have been very successful with a more family-oriented, holistic approach. They are more therapeutic in nature and incorporate such issues as addressing addiction and mental health concerns and rewarding positive behavior. These are now the options I advocate to parents like the hectoring perfectionist dad. I certainly hope he took my advice and changed his attitude when his girls returned home, but in reality, I would have to say that I doubt he did. The girls were fifteen and sixteen, only two or three years from the finish line to adulthood and freedom. They just have to hold on; the end is in sight.

Here's what I tell these parents, "I am a private investigator, and I am really good at what I do. Finding your child is the easy part. What's nearly impossible is undoing all the damage you have done over the past sixteen years in sixteen days."

* * *

In 2010, one of the most baffling disappearances in recent American history happened right in my own backyard. Joseph McStay, a well-liked fountain designer with his own successful business, simply vanished from his suburban Fallbrook, California, home. So did his wife Summer and their two young sons, aged three and four. Joseph's brother, unable to reach them, eventually broke into the house. He found no signs of disorder or foul play, but evidence that the family had left in a hurry: food on the counter, half-eaten bowls of popcorn in the living room, the family's two beloved dogs unfed in the backyard.

Theories abounded: they had voluntarily moved to Mexico to start over; a vengeful former boyfriend of Summer's had abducted them; they were the victims of a vicious drug cartel. In the course of the investigation, the police located the family car, abandoned near the Mexican border. They reviewed film of border crossings around the time of the disappearance and turned up a tantalizing piece of video. In the grainy clip, a couple holding hands with two small children walked across the border in the middle of the night and vanished. This evidence was highly convincing and threw the investigation onto a single-track path. Law enforcement was 100 percent convinced that these people were the McStay parents and their two boys.

Active "investigation" into other areas pretty much ceased once that footage was uncovered. Going forward, the police assumed that the family had chosen to disappear into a foreign country. There was no telling what happened after they crossed that border. They could have easily run into trouble, been murdered and buried, and never, ever heard from again. This family had vanished without a trace.

Several months after the family disappeared, a member of the McStay family contacted me to bring me up to date on the investigation. Of course, I was already well aware of the case as it was huge local news. "Is there more you can do for us?" he asked. "I understand that you're an expert in missing persons cases, as well as one of the few investigators who have people in Mexico." I am proud of the fact that we are one of the very few PI agencies with boots on the ground in Mexico, a feat that took six years to set up (see http://www.investigatormexico.com). Those are in addition to our office in San Diego, which is frequently engaged on cases out of neighboring Tijuana.

Law enforcement appeared to be on top of the case. They would come under some heavy fire later, but at the time, they seemed to have done a good job with a vexing mystery. There had been no ransom demand, which I took as a bad sign. I was pretty sure the family was still down in Mexico, but I was not sure what exactly we could do. Run all around that huge country and look for them . . . everywhere? To get the Mexican police on the case, I'd have to start handing out hundred-dollar bills wherever I went; that's just the reality of how their system works.

The most important thing was to keep the case in the headlines and public interest high. No problem there; this mystery had captivated not only Southern California but the entire nation. I told the McStay relative that keeping a high profile was the best course of action I could advise and offered to help them unofficially, free of charge, as an advisor, which I did, though nothing ever came of it and no arrests were ever made. Really, my role was that of a cheerleader for the family. I did my best to comfort them, advise them, and encourage them. Looking back, I am glad I didn't take the case, because as it turned out, there was sadly nothing anybody could have done. Joseph, Summer, and their sons were dead long before anyone ever had an inkling they were missing.

Three full years after the family vanished, four sets of bones were discovered in shallow graves by a motorcyclist in the Mojave Desert near Victorville, California. They turned out to be the remains of the McStay family. It was yet another year before an arrest was made—Joseph's former business partner, a man named Chase Merritt. Merritt had a criminal record and was the last person to have spoken to Joseph before the family disappeared. Merritt really should have taken the time to dig just a little deeper. Another foot, and those bodies would never have been discovered. Without bodies, law enforcement would never have further investigated this guy. He came this close to getting away with quadruple murder. The recriminations began immediately, of course.

Now, let me say that I abhor when armchair sleuths go back to second-guess what happened on a criminal case . . . what shoulda, coulda, woulda been done. Unless you were actually there, it's just not fair to try to second-guess what happened. Given the benefit of hindsight, it's easy to look back and ask . . . just how carefully was the videotape analyzed? Was it sent to the FBI to be compared against other video of the family? Was every enhancement technology used? At the first inspection of the house, what exactly did you see? Where is the crime scene analysis? And, most importantly, why wasn't Merritt checked out within an inch of his life?

Believe me, I get the outrage: this guy was Joseph McStay's coworker. A friend of the family. An ex-con. The last person known to have seen the family. I can see that it would be very easy to jump on the bandwagon condemning the investigation when it eventually came out that he was the murderer—and an extremely brutal one, to boot. In business or money disputes, one person usually kills the other person and that's it. They might possibly kill the spouse too. But two small helpless boys? Come on. Merritt was in an absolutely insane fit of rage; this was a classic case of overkill. However, he had an alibi and did a masterful job throwing law enforcement off the trail.

The main takeaway from this murder masquerading as a mystery? Something that I hope I've made clear throughout this book. Interview and interrogation skills are the most important qualities a good private investigator can have. Sadly, it is also the number one skill lacking in law enforcement today.

Watch an episode of *20/20* or *Dateline* or any of those popular mystery crime shows. So many stories are about wrongly convicted people and overturned convictions. So many miscarriages of justice could be avoided if law enforcement had proper interview and interrogation skills in the very beginning!

I've been on the job for thirty years. For the last six, I've worked as a detective in the Missing Persons Unit, and it's exactly where I want to be. It's not the first area officers gravitate to when they join the police department. Most people did not become cops to work disappearances. They want action: murder, robbery, drugs; those sorts of crimes are where their priorities lie. I have always been interested in missing persons; I like to follow the twists and turns in a disappearance to see where it leads. In Missing Persons, our unit of four detectives uses all the resources at our command to try to solve these mysteries. We do everything in our power to locate the person and hopefully bring some answers and relief to family and friends.

The single biggest misconception the general public has about missing persons is that they are required to wait twenty-four hours to report someone missing. That has never been an official rule. The reality is that you can call or come in to the station anytime to file a missing persons report. Obviously, the sooner the better: the first twenty-four hours of a missing persons case are crucial should it turn out to be a crime. You can make your report over the telephone, but I would always advise that you show up in person and bring along with a current photograph of the missing person.

Once the report is taken, the officer has two hours to enter the information into the National Crime Information Center (NCIC), which is a nationwide database. From that point on, law enforcement anywhere in the country can track somebody if they are stopped, no matter where they started or how far away they end up. Here are some key things to keep in mind as you go to file a missing persons report:

- Be persistent. Missing persons reports are long and complicated and per the rules must be entered into the system within two hours of taking the information. Therefore, not all officers on duty will be particularly anxious to jump in and get involved. Be polite but firm, and don't leave until an officer has taken your full report.
- Be accurate. It is crucial for you and the officer to be as accurate as possible with your reporting. Date of birth, height and weight, eye color, and especially spelling are so important. If a nickname goes into the NCIC system instead of a person's real name, even if they're detained, their name won't pop up. Do not let the officer taking the report assume anything when it comes to spelling names, such as Smythe versus the more ordinary Smith. Because of errors like this, people wait in vain for years for news on a missing person when he or she has been detained several times. The onus is on you as the reporting person to give the correct information, and check to make sure it is right.
- Follow up. Get the name and contact information of a missing persons detective before you leave. Call the station several hours after you return home to follow up and be sure the name was correctly entered into the NCIC system and the report and photograph were forwarded to a missing persons detective. Call the detective yourself if you don't hear from them soon. Things should start to move from here.

This is what happens on our end: I will make contact with the reporting person and get all the relevant information I can to work the case. The reality is that I average 100 new cases per month, so some prioritizing is absolutely necessary. Some missing persons quickly return home on their own, which is great; we just remove them from the system and close the report. Many missing persons suffer from mental illness, so we might find them in shelters or homeless encampments. Others might be found because they have been a victim of foul play, meaning the case now becomes a homicide. Some really seem to disappear into thin air.

We take the photo and make flyers right away. I have had amazing luck locating people throughout the years with flyers, even in these days where social media predominates. We post the information on the missing persons section of our website. We follow the leads provided by friends and family. In short, we do everything we can to find that person.

Cletus Carlton

Detective, Adult Missing Persons Unit

8

BRINGING PEOPLE TOGETHER

By the year 2000, Martin Investigative Services was nearing its third decade in business and going strong. In addition to my original office in Orange County, I had established satellite offices in Los Angeles and San Diego and was using fourteen investigators, all former federal agents like myself.

My proprietary database held more than 4 billion bits of information and was growing every day. The Internet was just starting to really take off and change the world. Always a big believer in giving back, I now had more of both the means and reach to do so. When a local reporter phoned me in the spring requesting a routine interview about locating people, I accepted. I decided this was an ideal opportunity to help others.

A good part of any private investigator's time is spent tracking people down. By this time, I was a veteran people finder, with hundreds of satisfactory searches conducted for clients all over the country. With Mother's Day and Father's Day coming up, I decided I would offer free searches for both sides: mothers and fathers seeking children, and sons and daughters looking for parents. I expected many requests would come from those who were adopted or had given up children at birth, but also knew from experience there were many fractured families out there searching for "lost" members. Divorce, drug and/or alcohol issues, and bitter feuds were just a few of the reasons I'd seen families become estranged and fall completely out of touch.

I threw out my special offer to the *Orange County Register* readers, specifying to the reporter that I would give precedence to anyone who could offer us something to go on concerning their case. A date of birth, a last known address, Social Security number—we needed to begin with a nugget of information to give us a lead, no matter how small. The reporter finished up our talk, thanked me, and told me to look for the article a week from the following Sunday. I joined my parents for lunch on that date as it happened to be their anniversary. I brought the paper along to show them.

"Guess what?" I told them during dessert. "I'm in the paper today!" I pulled out the huge Sunday edition and started thumbing through every section. I finally found my interview buried way in the back, pretty much sandwiched between lawn care ads and lost pets classifieds. The text of the article was dwarfed by a huge unsmiling photo of me. I looked like a gangster.

"That's a terrible picture of you!" my mother said.

"I didn't get to pick it, Mom," I told her.

"Well, that's ridiculous," she said, and we were on to a discussion of stock photos and how interviews actually worked. I quickly scanned the article; it seemed fine. After we finished lunch, I stopped by the office on my way home to grab a file. I heard the phone ringing nonstop as I walked through the door. Our fax machine was practically smoking; page after page of thermal paper was scrolling and landing in the overflowing basket. The deluge of requests had begun.

In the next week, our new e-mail inboxes overflowed. The phones rang off the hook. Letter after letter complete with photos and copies of official records were dumped in the office every day; our mail carrier was less than pleased. When it was all said and done, more than three thousand requests had come in—3,338 to be exact. Instead of handling several searches, which was all I had expected, we took on ten cases, located all the subjects, then did ten more. All the subjects were successfully found.

To say I was overwhelmed by this response would be an understatement. A few weeks later, just as things were settling down, a statistic in an article I happened to read in *US News and World Report* jumped out at me: *80 percent of Americans are currently looking for somebody.* That was, the magazine cautioned, a conservative estimate. Seeing that number, on top of my recent experience, really galvanized me. I thought, I've really got to get something going. So I did. I established my own toll-free phone number (888-USUNITE/888-878-6483) and website to help anyone searching for someone.

The site http://www.888USUNITE.com combined a number of resources for searchers. It hosted several free and low-cost search engines, allowing users to search by name, city, e-mail address, and numerous other factors. It searches for data from public and commercial databases, phone records, employment and corporate information, real estate transactions, and many other public records. As social media came into play, we also linked to Facebook and other popular sites to aid in the search. The idea was to provide help to not just private citizens but the business community as well. I wanted to become the go-to resource for anyone seeking to find anyone, including those who could not afford the services of a PI.

I believed then, and the research in the years since then has borne me out, that the average person has a 50 percent success rate finding the person they seek with a nominal amount of money spent. Of course, that means he or she devotes sufficient time and patience to the search and possesses knowledge of where to look. That, in a nutshell, is what www.888USUNITE.com was and still is all about. For the 49 percent who are not able to find their subject, the next step is a professional private investigator. The remaining 1 percent simply are not in mainstream America and will never be found. I say this not to brag, but simply as a fact: If we can't find the person, no one can.

Let's say you are a probate attorney settling a complicated will. You have been charged with locating five beneficiaries named in the trust, meaning you must do a due-diligence search to find each one. Retaining the services of a first-class investigator to handle these searches will go a long way toward settling your case.

If we at Martin Investigative Services are unable to find a given person, we will sign a declaration on penalty of perjury, under the laws of California or whatever state we find ourselves in, that no more time or money would be helpful in locating this person. All avenues of inquiry have been exhausted. In other words, we could not find them, and no one else will either. Most courts will accept this declaration and exclude that person. The heirs will now officially and legally split the assets four ways.

Another example: let's say you're just trying to track down an old military buddy or childhood friend. You retain us to find him or her after doing your best to locate them with no luck. If we don't find them, we will return your money. We are that confident in our work product. We have a 100 percent money-back guarantee on every case we accept, no questions asked. Let's discuss the ways you can maximize your—and our—chances of success in finding that person you seek.

My office receives probably three or four calls a *day* from people seeking their birth parents. Ninety-five percent of them don't have any information whatsoever about them; they only know who their adoptive parents are. If you are just starting out and know nothing, your adoptive parents are less than forthcoming, and you have absolutely no documentation of anything, there's nothing I can do for you. I sympathize, and I'd like to help, but please, do your homework before calling an investigator!

I will always start with a request for very basic information: Do you have a copy of your birth certificate? Do you know who handled the adoption . . . a private lawyer, an agency, a social worker? Without somewhere to start, there's no point in us taking your money; turning down these searchers is the most frustrating part of adoption work, bar none. Our in-house computer program is state of the art. But I need something to trace back!

Before you engage a PI, I highly recommend having a frank talk with your adoptive parents. Tell them that you would like to connect with your birth parents and that you hope they will assist you in your search. Parents are sometimes hesitant to share this information; some worry that once their child finds their birth parent, they'll be discarded like yesterday's Kleenex. A generally unfounded fear, by the way.

Nearly every person I have ever known who is adopted simply wants to know . . . What did my mother look like? What were the circumstances of my birth? Why did she give me up? Even though they may have a wonderful life, been given every advantage, and deeply love their parents, there is still a deep curiosity in human beings to understand where they come from. Others have a more pressing need to find out medical information when they have an illness with a genetic component or want to start their own families. Finding that birth parent will hopefully bring a sense of finality and closure in their lives.

The truth of the matter is that finding birth parents, or a child given up for adoption, is a relatively easy thing to do depending on the state where the birth took place and the person hired to help track them down. It's a matter of knowing how the system works. If you are adopted, you have a birth certificate with your adoptive parent or parents' name on it. That certificate has a number, which corresponds to actual original birth records from hospitals. We find the *original* birth certificate with the birth mom and dad's names on it, then try to locate the father. Males are generally easier to find, because their name remains the same. Mothers have more than likely married or remarried and changed their surnames. That's the short and simple explanation . . . now you have to find somebody who knows how to correlate that number with the first original live birth certificate. This is where a skilled investigator comes in.

When somebody comes into my office and says, "I was given up for adoption and want to hire you to find my birth parents," here is how it works. Some cases we rule out right away, because they occurred in states with historically poor record keeping. If we agree to take the case, I will find your birth mother and/or father, with one caveat: If and when they tell me they don't want to meet you, I will not disclose their names or contact information.

I am one of the few private detectives in the country who goes by this rule. This is a caveat that doesn't even occur to most private eyes; many will just e-mail a name, address, and phone number to the client and let them do what they will with it. I deplore this tactic; I consider it an invasion of privacy. I am strongly for the "right to know" of anyone searching for their birth parents. But there is a right way and a wrong way to go about things.

When I track down a birth parent, I've gotten every reaction from "I've been waiting for this day for decades" and tears of joy to absolute stone-cold refusal to even consider seeing their child. Birth parents, once found, present a very interesting set of dynamics. Many of these men and women have settled into new relationships, often stable long-term marriages with children, but never told their mates about their adopted baby. Talk about throwing a grenade into a marriage! What often happens is the father will only agree to one secret meeting; they don't want their spouse to know.

It's all in how you approach the person. I have never once in thirty-five years been turned down, because we know how to best handle this very delicate situation. Most of the men who have fathered a child think he or she is coming after them for money or financial support, so we dispel that notion right away. We immediately establish the child is not seeking money. I have met many birth parents who start out saying "Under no circumstances do I want any part of this!" But I keep at it . . . politely. I do my best to convince them. "This is not going to be a long, enduring relationship. Can I just show you a picture? You know, you have grandchildren . . . how about I just leave these photos with you." Usually they'll consent to look at photos. I then reapproach and say, "Will you consider having just one short meeting at a restaurant or public place of your choosing with him or her?"

What I always tell the birth mother or father is that the son or daughter given up for adoption twenty-eight years ago hired me to find you, and I did. If they refuse to consider any contact, I ultimately say that I will honor the request and respect their right to privacy. However, if I was able to find them, someone else could too. And the next investigator might not be so discreet. Let's just put this matter behind us, I urge them. You don't want someone showing up on your doorstep . . . so let's do this the easy way, with whatever restrictions you want to place on the meeting.

I find this a vastly preferable scenario to just handing over a name and address to the client. That is when a nightmare begins. I've had at least fifty cases where a man or woman who has been "found" calls me in a panic. "I just got a call from a private investigator . . . he said the daughter I gave up for adoption twenty-two years ago is now married and living in Missouri and wants to meet me . . . my husband knows nothing about her! What do I do?" Just so you know, if this might be your situation, it's a terrible idea to get someone's number and call to say . . . "Hi? This is Mary, birthdate November 18, 1984 . . . I got your number from a PI . . . I think you're my dad . . . call me on my cell." As you can imagine, people go absolutely nuts.

Again, I believe this kind of intrusion is a real violation. Anyone who gave up a child for adoption certainly had their reasons. Someone who tried to do the right thing legally, signed the papers, and went on with their own life without interfering in their birth child's does not deserve to have their entire existence blown up twenty or thirty years later. In these cases, I work backward. I quickly reach out to the searcher who left the message and say, "Listen, you are not going about this in the best way. Please call me, and let's talk about facilitating a meeting with my client."

In the meantime, I am simply grateful my client got the message instead of the spouse or one of their kids. Reunions are high-drama situations at best, but I am not here to ruin anyone's life. I always hope for happy endings!

In a twist on the usual tale, I once had a mother come to me seeking the daughter she had given up for adoption at birth some twenty-five years before. Once I located the young woman, she agreed to come to my office for a meeting. As we sat and chatted, we realized that she had been on my daughter's swim team ten years earlier. We had a great talk. Then she dropped a bombshell. "You know I have three biological sisters, right?" she asked.

"What?" I said.

"Yes, my mom gave up all four of us for adoption at the same time. We were two, three, four, and six. I was the three-year-old."

Now that was news to me. When I called my client later to report on our meeting, I asked about the existence of three other daughters. She sighed and said, "Yeah, I had four daughters."

"Why didn't you tell me about all of them?"

"I thought you would think I was a bad mother."

I don't make judgments. I find people! I proceeded to locate her other three daughters as well, and they had a big reunion at a restaurant in Anaheim. All four daughters had turned out wonderfully, happily married, some with children, and all doing very well in life. My client got to meet seven grandchildren. Now that's the kind of ending I like to see!

As a full-service, all-around private investigator, I take on all kinds of cases. My biggest strength lies in interview and interrogation, which are paramount in this profession. I have a pleasant personality; I never come off aggressively or try to intimidate anyone. You can get a lot of doors slammed in your face in this business; when I approach people, I can usually at least get them to listen to me for a minute. Long enough to believe that I'm an honest broker who's truly interested in hearing their side of the story. The subject might tell me things my client doesn't particularly want to hear, but I write them down accurately and report that information nonetheless. The truth is what my clients need, pleasant or not.

Because of this skill, I often do litigation support for attorneys and work for corporate clients. At this stage of the game—I've been an investigator for forty-eight years—I only handle high-end surveillances that require extensive coverage. In the business world, this would include corporate espionage cases, where an executive may be secretly meeting with competitors and selling trade secrets or planning to leave their firm and take all the clients. In other words, the sort of situation that requires a good couple weeks of round-the-clock surveillance.

Then there are the personal cases, where I am asked to find/do surveillance on family members. Many people who go missing have mental health issues. Throwing illegal drug use on top of psychiatric problems is gasoline on a fire. Often, I am contacted to track down children over the age of eighteen. As official adults, these young people are free to do as they please. Parents cannot put them into any type of facility against their will or force them into rehab or a facility or make them stay on their meds. They certainly can't make them stay home. These young adults are just out there, lost.

I am going to share two stories of lost "children" that have stuck with me through the years. Both of these young people came from extremely affluent families. However, their wealth did not guarantee ease or happiness. These parents, however, did have the funds for extensive investigation services, which hopefully provided peace of mind. Sometimes, that's the most you can ask for.

When locating someone, I always start with the last known sighting of the person as the starting point. I take a clear recent photo with me, then get out there and do the old-fashioned footwork. Shelters and informants tend to be quite helpful. However, in this digital age, I can often track young adults by purchases on their debit cards or credit cards that are billed to their parents. That was the case for both of these kids.

I was contacted by an extremely affluent family in New York City about their son, who until recently had been a student. He suffered from some mental health issues and had quit school to take off across the country and live in Berkeley in a rough neighborhood near the university. He was still living off a credit card billed to them, so they could track his moves. They hired me to do a week of full-time surveillance. The former student was living in a seedy motel room; he only left twice a day—once to buy food at a local taqueria and later to buy drugs on a street corner. The rest of his time he spent in his room, doing drugs and listening to music. A couple times, however, he rented a car and drove recklessly around the city. As we tailed him, he was an absolute menace on the road, very nearly causing a few accidents. All this was clearly documented in our daily reports and video clips.

My clients were working closely with a psychiatrist in their home state of New York; we were sending our reports to the parents and the psychiatrist every night. By the end of the week, they had sufficient evidence from our reporting that he was a clear danger to himself and others. The psychiatrist and the boy's parents flew out west, hired a local attorney, and got a court order to bring their son back to New York to be treated. He was put away in a hospital for a time, but a couple years later killed himself. There's not always a happy ending in this business.

Another very rich family from New York hired me to find their daughter, who had become estranged from them. She was nineteen years old and had been educated in one of the most elite private schools in the city—so bright that she gained early admittance to Harvard. An eating disorder and drug issues derailed her in her senior year. She just hit the wall. Cindy began smoking pot all day and pretty much dropped out of life. Eventually, she left home when relations with her mom and dad got too frayed. Her frantic parents wanted us to locate her and follow her, mainly to ensure her safety.

We did find her in a very seedy neighborhood in Hollywood. Cindy was a lovely young lady who liked to smoke a lot of marijuana, and she would fearlessly enter the most terrible neighborhoods to buy it. As she was tiny, soft-spoken, and blond, this was a very dangerous habit. We were on the case for a couple of months, and all of us investigators on the case became quite attached to her, though we never spoke to her directly. Cindy was a sweet soul; she spent a great deal of time in metaphysical stores, following new age pursuits. The owners of one mystical bookstore basically adopted her and let her stay in a small rental room in the back of the property. Whenever she left, we were her guardians.

My associates, Bobby and David, and I were on surveillance one night at opposite ends of the street when all of a sudden I heard David yell in my earpiece, "Dammit, Cindy, don't go down that alley!"

"What's she doing?" I asked him.

"Heading toward a bunch of gang members in a dead-end alley!" I turned the corner just in time to see David jump in his car, turn on his brights, and head straight down the alley, scattering gang members left and right. Cindy watched in shock and walked away. She wasn't going to get any drugs that night.

Soon enough, Cindy got a job at a new age store on Melrose Avenue. David and I would shake our heads as we watched her close up shop at night. She would straighten out the bottles and shelves so carefully and took such good care of the stock. We couldn't help but think how her father would happily buy her an entire store of her own and put it in the Beverly Center if that's what she wanted to do! Her bosses, an elderly Hasidic couple, were also quite taken with her, and they watched out for her too. After nearly two months of constant surveillance, we were satisfied Cindy had arranged a fairly good routine for herself. We had been able to reassure her family during this time that she was safe enough . . . sometimes, thanks to us.

Eventually, her mother came out and met with the couple who employed her daughter on a day when Cindy wasn't there; they eventually convinced Cindy to consent to meet with her mother again. She eventually reconciled with her parents and returned to live in their palatial penthouse in New York. We were thrilled with this job; we kept a young woman safe, assured her parents that their daughter was okay during her absence, and eventually facilitated a reunion.

People might ask, why couldn't the parents just take the information we provided about where she was and go talk to her? Well, she wasn't ready at that point. She probably would have bolted again. Cindy's was the very best kind of ending for a missing young adult's case. This kind of resolution and reunion is what makes this job so gratifying.

John Marcello, Senior Investigator
Martin Investigative Services
Newport Beach, California

* * *

How do I find someone? Where to begin? It depends on the information you already have and what you're trying to find out. If you know the person's name and you're looking to reconnect, or simply find a current address, telephone number, or e-mail address, try these easily accessible sources:

- Social Media Sites—Start here, because these days most people and businesses have some sort of profile on at least one social network. The most prominent social networking sites such as Facebook, LinkedIn, Google+, and MySpace offer free search facilities of their pages by name, zip code, and e-mail address, although using them typically requires registration.
- Specialized Sites—If you'd like to try searches at a number of smaller social networking sites, Wikipedia maintains a full list of active social networking websites.
- Search Engines—Begin with the basics. Simple searches on highly trafficked search engines may guide you to the missing person's address and telephone number. The top four search engines by usage are Google, Yahoo, Bing, and Ask. By checking all four, you can obtain different results, since each engine has different data sets and ways of returning

results. When performing searches, remember to put your search phrase in quotation marks (e.g., "thomas martin") to improve the relevance of your results.

- 888-USUNITE—When it comes to sites dedicated to finding people, begin with http://www.888USUNITE.com, the site/toll-free number I founded. It hosts several free and low-cost search engines, including Zabasearch, 123people, Pipl, and Zoominfo, and also includes links to social media. The go-to resource for those seeking to find someone.

Several other helpful sites specifically for people searching are:

- Yahoo People Search/123People Search—a comprehensive free people-search engine
- Switchboard.com—an online directory of the telephone numbers and addresses of 100 million-plus Americans from white and yellow pages
- The New Ultimates—an invaluable site that assists with roughly 85 percent of our lookups; it lets you search twenty-five people-search resources in one spot
- Reunion.com—Reunion's network has a people-search engine and also connects former classmates with each other through a school search

Names may be unknown if you are looking for an adopted child or for birth parents. In these cases, your search will take more time while you contact everyone you think may have a piece of the puzzle: a relative, former neighbor, clergy, lawyer, or caseworker. Here is a list of sites you may find helpful for more specialized searches:

- The Federal Parent Locator Service is the section of the Federal Office of Child Support Enforcement's website that lists information, systems, and agencies available to those looking to locate participants in child support cases.

- Adoption.com's Reunion Registry and Adopt.com are two of the web's largest reunion websites for birth parents and adoptees, each boasting nearly half a million adoption records and registries for both parents and children seeking each other.
- Social Security Death Index—index to deaths recorded by the Social Security Administration since 1962.
- Rootsweb (rootsweb.com) Genealogical Data Cooperative Page—tracks surnames.
- The US Gen Web Project—a volunteer effort that offers advice on how to find basic genealogical data, such as local churches, cemeteries, and court, land, and property records. Each state has its own web page that lists phone numbers of local archives, genealogical societies, and libraries.
- National Archives and Records Administration—the nation's record keeper posts federal government records and helps users and researchers access ancestry information, military files, and much more.
- Ancestry.com—millions of vital records useful for research in genealogy, legal, family history, and the like.

9

PROTECTING YOUR HOME . . . AND EVERYTHING IN IT

By all accounts the brick mansion on Embassy Row near DC's National Cathedral was not only a showplace, but a truly happy home. A fifth-generation Washingtonian and proud Greek American, Savvas Savopoulos bought the sprawling property in 2002. He and his wife Amy raised two daughters and a son in the exclusive Georgetown enclave. A brilliant engineer, Savopoulos owned American Ironworks; after a career in accounting, Amy devoted herself to volunteer work and became a popular neighborhood hostess. In a city full of glittering parties every night, the couple was noted for their many philanthropic endeavors and charitable giving.

The first sign of trouble came when the local fire department responded to a call to the home on a mild Thursday afternoon in May. After dousing the blaze, firemen found four bodies inside: those of Savvas, Amy, their ten-year-old son Philip, and one of their housekeepers. The older daughters were away at boarding school. It was immediately apparent to authorities that the fire had been deliberately set. The blunt force trauma and marks of torture on several of the bodies sent the investigation into overdrive, as news crews from around the world descended on the tony neighborhood. Over the next seven days, a grim mystery played out in the once-beautiful home, now a partially burnt and flooded mess cordoned off from the street by yellow crime scene tape.

With no signs of forced entry, the killer was clearly someone known to the family and familiar with their routine. The family's long-time regular housekeeper reported that she had received a tense-sounding voicemail from Savvas on Wednesday night, telling her not to report for work as usual the next day. Domino's pizzas were delivered to the house that same night; the deliveryman picked up the money on the porch and left the boxes without interacting with anyone inside. Most chilling, Savvas's assistant had been directed by his boss to drop off $40,000 cash on their doorstep on Thursday. The bag holding the cash, along with the family's Porsche, vanished shortly before the fire began.

One week after the bodies were discovered, police tracked thirty-four-year-old Daron Wint to a motel in Maryland and, after a brief car chase, arrested him in DC in a truck filled with cash. Wint, a former employee of American Ironworks, had an extensive criminal record. His DNA had been found on pizza crusts in the home. Wint, along with several accomplices, including his brother, was quickly taken into custody. The former welder was eventually indicted on an array of charges including twelve counts of first-degree murder with "aggravating circumstances," indicating that the murders were especially "heinous, atrocious, or cruel."

The Department of Justice, in its press release announcing his indictment, formally praised the many law enforcement agencies and employees who had worked together on the speedy gathering of evidence and marshaling of charges against the suspect. As a former federal agent who has witnessed my own share of heinous crimes, I understood exactly how they felt. This was one of those scenes they would never forget, like the images in my mind of the tiny bodies of the McStay boys buried in the desert. A violent home invasion, being held captive and tortured and extorted for money, unable to protect your child from being hurt. Helpless in the place you should feel safest and most secure: this was truly the stuff of all of our very worst nightmares.

In the wake of this well-publicized quadruple homicide came the usual spate of articles and news stories: Would you survive a home invasion? Fortunately, this tragedy was given so much play in the media in part because of how rare these incidents are. Chances are slim to none this will ever happen, but for those who are worried, experts agree that the best thing to do is make a plan, rehearse it, and stick to it. The plan may be to try to flee, or to barricade yourself in a certain room.

Whatever the case, there needs to be an alarm word that when shouted over and over, every family member knows immediately where to try to run to and what to attempt to do.

However, in cases like that of the Savopoulos family, I must issue a caveat. Depending on the mental, physical, and spiritual qualities—or complete lack thereof—of the perpetrators involved, and exactly what their motive is, some people, sadly, simply don't stand a chance. When faced with predators of this nature, I don't care what security system you have or what precautions you have taken. When something this profoundly unexpected and violent happens to you, shock and adrenaline set in, and plans fly out the window. I wish I had the answer to preventing crimes like these. But as Mike Tyson so aptly said, "Everybody has a plan until they get punched in the face."

❖ ❖ ❖

It is heartening for us all to realize that, like a home invasion, the odds of a stranger kidnapping or molesting your child are small. In my world, I would say that 99 percent of both crimes are committed by someone known to the child, usually a parent (often estranged; more on that in a moment). When it comes to offering advice on keeping kids safe, I like to recommend the Polly Klaas Foundation website (http://www. pollyklaas.org). I am a fan of the work her father, advocate Marc Klaas, has done in the wake of his daughter's murder. This family has turned their notorious personal tragedy into good. They offer a wealth of information both on keeping children safe and what to do in the unlikely scenario of a stranger abduction.

If you visit their website, you will find information on how to report a missing child; they even provide you with your own caseworker. You can search their constantly updated master list of missing children, complete with photos, hometowns, and family contact information. You can request your free child safety kit, which will help you be prepared in the event of the unthinkable with a record of your child's fingerprints, DNA, and health information. I encourage you to join the nearly half million parents who have gotten this kit; meanwhile, as you browse, I would also encourage you to make a small donation to this very worthy charity, which has earned five stars from Charity Navigator.

nother resource for parents: Kidpower (http://www.kidpower.org) teaches positive skills to younger children, teenagers, and adults to prevent bullying, kidnapping, and other forms of abuse and violence. They also offer numerous helpful articles about keeping children safe and up-to-date statistics on violence against young people. Take a look.

* * *

I used to commit residential burglaries—purely for educational purposes, of course. As a PI, I was often asked to appear on local television shows about home security. In these segments, which were prearranged with news show producers, I would force my way into the home, which immediately set off the alarm. I would then call the nearest Domino's and order a pizza. Then I'd head into the master bedroom, grab a pillowcase, find all the jewelry, clean out the nightstand, and get out fast. Then I'd wait out front with my bag of loot. It made for great TV as I sat on the stoop, waiting to see who would arrive first. Cops or pizza? Pizza came first, every single time.

I always tell people that an alarm is just the first basic step in home security. You should never rely too heavily on the response from any alarm company, even the very best. In the old days, when I used to do these TV demos, it used to cost five or six thousand dollars to wire a house for security purposes, with monitoring fees running several hundred dollars every month. Given all the advances in technology, you can now install state-of-the-art wireless security for a few hundred bucks, with monitoring running something like $15 a month. With all the new web-based systems, you can monitor your own cameras online and handle security all by yourself from a phone or laptop if you choose.

What I'd like to stress is that all of the electronic systems and gear are high-quality these days. Remember, it's not how good your system is, it's how good the monitoring is. Now, if the alarm is disabled or there's no alarm system to begin with, that's when burglars really go to town. They can check out your refrigerator, have a drink, wander around, and take their time. However, most professional burglars don't linger. They know that once they hear that alarm go off, they have ninety seconds. They need to get in and out. Most professionals are going to bet that if the alarm goes off, the police are coming. They'll abandon their mission and go to the next house with no alarm . . . or barking dog.

Here is a startling statistic for you: of the 500 residential burglary investigations we have conducted during the past three decades throughout the United States, our case files reflect that 80 percent of those burglaries occurred in a home with a security system that was not turned on. The largest residential burglary ever in the state of California happened in the city of Tustin in Orange County. The family got taken for millions and millions of dollars' worth of cash and valuables. They had a very sophisticated alarm . . . it just wasn't turned on. This is simply a matter of people becoming complacent, or lazy.

An alarm system is an excellent first line of defense. But how can it work if you don't bother to set it? Arming and disarming your house must become second nature to you and every member of your household. The code must be changed frequently for security purposes. I never thought one of my best tips to prevent burglary would be, "Set your alarm," but there you have it.

Many high-end homes these days have built-in safes in a closet, or people spend a great deal of money on fireproof, indestructible safes that weigh a ton. These are great for preserving important papers and records; not so great for security. A safe can be broken into; any code can be cracked. In the old days, people used to hide valuables in the pantry, in fake Pringles cans. That's really old school. There are much better ways.

Let's say you are lucky enough to own a Mariah Carey kind of engagement ring . . . you know, twenty carats or so. The kind of bauble you're not going to wear out to the supermarket every day. Where are you going to store it? A safe is the first place burglars will look. I recommend that people locate an electrical socket in an-out-of-the way part of the house that's not being used. Get a handyman to remove the plate and plug and wiring and cut a small box inside the wall. Then reinstall the plate back over the hole, and tell no one about it. Trust me, no one will ever find your valuables in a million years.

I urge you to do this now, because should your home be burglarized, chances that your valuables will be recovered are slim to none. We get two or three calls a week in our offices from people whose homes have been burglarized. We are always candid and transparent, right from the start, about what we can and cannot do. The cash is gone, never to be seen again. The jewelry is also gone. Most professional thieves who steal jewelry have a place to fence their loot. They take the stolen jewelry to another crook who pays them ten cents on the dollar, if they're lucky. The jeweler melts down the gold and uses the diamonds in other pieces that he sells.

Callers often ask us to conduct a search for their jewelry in pawnshops. These days, laws are very strict. Pawnshop employees take fingerprints and a copy of your driver's license before they'll agree to take anything you have, so forget searching pawnshops—nobody does that anymore. Your stolen items won't turn up there.

So what can a private investigator do after the fact? If your claim is over fifty thousand dollars, you might want to hire one to investigate. Our agency can help in three ways. With a private investigator on the case, it is much more likely that your report will rise to the top of the pile in a very busy law enforcement office. Hopefully, your PI will give the detectives some more incentive to work on your case—one of the many, many residential burglary reports they receive each week.

Secondly, an investigator can bring his or her interview and interrogation skills to bear and speak to any suspects the person may have. Usually, people have some thoughts about who might have committed the burglary. An interview by a first-class PI can help shed some light on the matter. Finally, if you are making an insurance claim of any kind, hiring an investigator usually helps the process go smoothly. When the insurance company sees such action on your part, they realize you are serious about this claim and generally pay up promptly and with very little questioning.

Home security has changed radically in the twenty years I've been working in this business. During the great housing boom of the 2000s, before the whole real estate market crashed, more people than ever before were installing security systems, but they were buying them blindly. Thousands of people signed on the dotted line without paying much attention to the fine print or what kind of service they were getting. These days, consumers are much better educated. In addition, the advent of wireless technology was a game-changer. The whole security alarm business is heading toward cellular technology and automation: controlling home systems on a phone or tablet from anywhere in the world. It's an exciting time to be in this field.

My true love has always been sales. My dad was a highly successful salesperson for AT&T and Lucent Technologies, and I wanted to do what he did: get out there, see the world, and sell. I love talking to people and helping them. I had friends who were police officers, and I had a degree in criminal justice; the security industry was a natural fit for me. I took a job as a salesperson right out of school. Many alarm companies only specialize in one system or one type of security; Safe-T Security offered every kind of system available. My knowledge base grew really fast. After two decades, I'm now the company sales director. Salespeople are not generally known to have great knowledge of the technical side of the business. Here at Safe-T, I am continually trained on all the new technologies, so I really know what I'm selling and installing.

I am never worried about just what I can sell someone; my primary concern is to help clients regain their footing and peace of mind. We are often called immediately after a client has undergone a traumatic experience: a break-in, home invasion, or burglary; they may have been stalked; whatever the dangerous situation may be that has led them to need our services. Though our actual job is to install security systems, we are dealing with very sensitive matters and the personal touch really matters.

The biggest myth about security is believing that if you install a good security system, your house is 100 percent safe and everything is good from here on out. Unfortunately, in this world there are no guarantees, only deterrents. A security system will offer you a certain level of comfort—hopefully a pretty high one. We can't promise our security system will stop a break-in, but we certainly believe it will deter many attempts. In addition to an alarm system, everyone needs to examine the other security features in their life. Do you leave porch lights on at night? Are your bushes cut back so the view of the yard is clear? Do you leave trash cans out and let the mail stack up for days when you're away, so it's very obvious that no one is home? So many factors come into play; having a solid security system is just one important component in the process.

We are called to the scene of many burglaries, and one of the newer trends is that criminals are paying attention to other people's schedules and planning break-ins around them. Here in Southern California, there is constant construction, remodeling, and home improvement going on all the time. There are lots of temporary workers around, constantly, on every street in Los Angeles. Transient workers on a job, or their friends, easily get a good idea of local residents' schedules; they see the cars coming and going at regular times. They can pretty much estimate how long a homeowner will be gone after being on a residential street working in the yard for a week.

More break-ins happen nowadays in the daytime than in the nighttime. Just last week, one of the moms from the soccer team I coach called me to her house in the morning. She literally drove her kid to school, dropped him off, and returned to a ransacked house. She was only gone for twenty minutes, but that's when her home got hit. Whoever broke in saw her leave and knew that they had a solid twenty minutes where they would be unbothered. It was as predictable as clockwork; she made the same run every day. Something for everybody to keep in mind.

So what should you do to ensure your safety? Everyone is different; people have vastly varying ideas on what makes them personally feel "safe." When you come into your house at the end of the workday, or turn out the lights just before you go to sleep at night, what will it take to give you a sense of security and calm? Maybe it's just locking your doors and windows or having a dog—that's plenty for lots of people. Many others don't even go that far—they habitually leave their doors unlocked because they live in "safe" or "nice" neighborhoods . . . though that's not something I recommend.

Plenty of old-school people still like a yard sign announcing there's a security system. I tell everyone that any form of security is better than none. I even like putting a prominent "Beware of Dog" sign on your gate, whether or not you have a dog. We can install wireless motion lights along the driveway, so if someone is coming toward your home in the dark, they'll trip the light and maybe a neighbor will notice. Keeping a car parked in the driveway every now and then instead of inside the garage is a good idea.

There are many, many ways to deter break-ins, and a reputable security company is here to help you throw around every idea. Before something happens to you, identify what your personal safety zone is. If what is going to make you happiest is the very latest alarm, complete with cameras and twenty-four-hour surveillance, then by all means look into it.

People used to be scared of security systems back in the old days. They thought they were too difficult to program; they were confusing; the alarms would go off at the wrong time. These days they are so simple to set and use; it's just punching in a four-digit code or hitting an off-button on a keyring. Camera systems are becoming an increasingly important component in home security; if people think they are being watched, they are far less likely to commit crimes. When an intruder hears an alarm go off, they know they have ten minutes before the police get there or the residents come racing home. They are far more likely to not break in at all if they know someone is pulling up video on their smartphone in real time and watching them in the home. That footage can then be shown to the police. Visual evidence is what law enforcement likes to see to make a case. Cameras are definitely the next wave of the business.

I am frequently called to install camera systems for neighbors who don't get along. I am amazed at how many old-time kind of Hatfield and McCoy feuds are going strong today in every kind of neighborhood. People call all the time saying, "We think our neighbor is stealing our fruit . . . harming our dog . . . taking our mail" . . . you name it. They want cameras installed to catch someone in the act. That is currently one of our most popular requests. People are watching television shows, observing cameras where they work, or just learning through word of mouth—even people who've never had any kind of security before request cameras.

Normally, in these cases we then post a sign saying "These premises monitored by video." Technically, you have to tell people they're being recorded—even robbers. The more signage you have of any kind, the better. Some people don't want a security sign in their front yard because they're looking to catch somebody in the act. We have to retrain them into a better way of thinking.

The odds of catching someone are very poor. The odds of deterring somebody and having them just move on to a different house are very strong. And that's the whole idea of security, isn't it?

We deal with every income level in this business, and I understand that price is an issue when it comes to security. Unfortunately, there are some really bad contracts out there in the security world. Do your research, get some quotes, and do keep in mind that price isn't everything. Getting the lowest monthly monitoring rate is not necessarily the best thing or only consideration. What does saving $15 a month mean when you can't count on someone responding in a timely manner when the alarm goes off? In order to feel truly safe, you need to have a high level of confidence in your security provider.

Mike Kebelbeck, Sales Director
Safe-T Security Services
Riverside, California

Recommending that you hire a handyman to create a custom hiding place brings me to another important issue: being smart about the contractors and service people you let into your home. It's ideal if you can get a recommendation from a friend or family member, but these days, people move around a great deal, and they also turn to the Internet for everything. With that in mind, let's discuss a few of the most popular nationwide options out there.

Angie's List (Angieslist.com) has been around for nearly two decades. The company started when an Ohio woman was searching for a reputable contractor for her boss, and now has more than one million "pros" of all kinds on its list, including health care providers and mechanics. The company uses a proprietary vetting process, ensuring that its 10 million-plus reviews are authentic and that service providers cannot rate themselves highly or competitors poorly. Even so, be advised that companies that advertise on Angie's List have more exposure than those that don't, and nearly 70 percent of the company's revenues come from advertising, not membership fees. Angie's List is a subscription-based service costing about $11/year.

Homeadvisor (Homeadvisor.com) is a free service matching homeowners with remodeling professionals in every area: bathrooms, drywall, electrical, landscaping/gardening, roofing, complete remodeling, and the like. When you put in the job you are looking to have done, the company matches you with local professionals who are free to do your job. The pros pay an annual membership fee and are not able to buy advertising or "pay their way" to the top. The site's helpful "true cost guide" offers detailed cost estimates for hundreds of possible jobs.

Porch.com's motto is "Don't DIY . . . Use Our Guys." This free site also matches homeowners to local remodeling pros. The site stands out because of its photos and descriptions of nearly 140 million home projects that help users get design/remodeling ideas and determine what their own budget will bear. Their app offers users free advice from various professionals and access to Better Business Bureau ratings for each provider.

Finally, a word about the BBB . . . or bbb.org online, a resource that is checked by more than 100 million consumers each year. Though it now offers user reviews, it is not a crowdsourced review site like the ones listed above. A company gets a profile with the BBB when a customer makes an official complaint . . . something that nearly one million Americans are moved to do each year. A company's rating (with grades like a report card, from A to F) is determined by how fast the company responds to a complaint and whether or not the dispute is resolved.

The news show *20/20* did a devastating expose on the company in 2010 called "The Best Ratings Money Can Buy,"[1] accusing the nonprofit organization of awarding good grades to those who paid "membership" fees, basically. In response, the company promised a number of reforms, including that the ratings system would no longer give more points or better scores to those who were accredited, as well as an investigation into BBB sales practices. Having dealt with overzealous reps from the BBB many times myself over the years, I will simply say by all means, check the site, but take their "grades" with a grain of salt.

There's only one review site I personally put any credence in, and that's Google+Local reviews. Forget Yelp and all the others. Here's why I say that: To post a review, users must have a Google+ profile, which are nearly always under a person's actual name and pretty much eliminates the fake review problem—both fake positives written by vendors

---

1. "Terror Group Gets 'A' From Better Business Bureau?" ABC News. November 12, 2010,http://www.abcnews.go.com/Blotter/business-bureau-best-ratings-money-buy/story?id=12123843.

to puff up their own business or fake negatives posted to bring down competitors. I can easily click to read someone's reviews to see if they have an axe to grind and what kind of reviews they tend to write; also just to make sure they're more or less on my wavelength in terms of what they're looking for and the level of service they expect.

When I'm out of town and looking for a service, I will check out the business, and if they don't have any Google reviews, then I won't use them. Businesses establish their own profiles, as well; Martin Investigative Services has one. I never push it or ask for a review, but if a client e-mails or tells me personally how happy she is with our work and wants to give us a good recommendation, there's a link we send to them. The whole process of reviewing on Google+Local is admittedly somewhat of a pain, but I like it. I know it's real!

HIGHLY RECOMMENDED

With the popularity of Internet shopping, daily deliveries to homes and small businesses seven days a week are now not a rarity, but the norm. The convenience of delivery to your door, of course, is a boon to professional thieves, who target unattended packages year-round, but especially during the holiday season.

It comes as no surprise that online behemoth Amazon.com is leading the charge for new solutions. Their Amazon Locker system allows customers to bypass home delivery altogether and pick up packages at nearby stations. These Amazon kiosks are located in stores where Amazon rents space and are open twenty-four-hours—7-Eleven has nearly 200 in various locations all over the country. Customers are notified by e-mail when a package has been delivered to their locker. They take their unique pickup code to the locker, enter it on the touch screen, and retrieve their package. Currently, the Amazon Locker is available in a number of East and West Coast major markets and continues to expand.

Other companies are coming up with innovative solutions to theft, missed deliveries, and inconvenient trips to pick up packages as well. The startup Doorman.com has vowed to fix how we receive online purchases once and for all in three very busy markets. They fill a special niche for busy urban dwellers, especially appreciated during the holidays. In a nutshell, customers have their items delivered to the company's package center, and then choose a convenient time for delivery (anytime from six until midnight, seven days a week). Doorman.com uses private contractors for the deliveries rather than regular drivers and rigorously controls for friendliness and reliability.

Currently, the service is just $4 per package, although they have a $20-a-month deal for those who have a large number of packages. This could be a better option for the holidays. Right now, the company only serves San Francisco, Chicago, and New York, though they are planning to expand.

A company from Portland, Oregon, called Landport has another potential solution (http://www.thelandport.com). Company founder Jody Pettit describes on the company website her disappointment at having a package containing a one-of-a-kind family heirloom stolen from her porch. The loss inspired her to create the Landport: an attractive, custom-made lockbox that comes in three sizes, suitable for both businesses and homeowners. Since the boxes are large and can be bolted down, they are unlikely to be carried away. Each box has a unique access code; delivery drivers simply enter the code and leave the box for you to pick up at your convenience. Buyers simply have to provide this code to their delivery company. As the company is in "the receiving business," they work with all delivery companies, including FedEx, UPS, and the USPS.

* * *

When it comes to my business clients, I strongly recommend that many of them have us check for hidden video and audio eavesdropping devices in the interest of corporate security (see http://www. bugsweepteam.com). This is known as electronic eavesdropping detection sweeps in our business—or "bug sweeps" to the general public. Any business whose staff routinely discusses sensitive or confidential information in a boardroom or other on-site location, or works on top-secret, proprietary projects, should conduct a sweep every three months. Certainly, never more than six months should go by without a thorough sweep. They should also be done for special circumstances, like just before a major board or shareholders meeting. For such organizations, the cost of regularly scheduled bug sweeps is minimal compared to the alternative of leaked information to competitors.

Back in the early days of my private investigative business, there wasn't much in the way of sophisticated equipment available to the average person to be able to bug somebody. The detection equipment was pretty primitive as well. I would estimate that we used to find bugs 3–4 percent of the time. Things began to change in the late eighties, after the Seoul Olympics. Many Americans traveled to Seoul to see the Summer Games and were fascinated by all kinds of cool electronic spy gadgets that were available there in electronics stores and on street corners. They brought them home, and ever since, there's been a huge influx of every kind of different listening device, monitor, receiver, remote, camera . . . you name it.

Soon enough, smartphones came along as well; now, every single citizen has a recorder and movie camera with them at all times. It's easy to tape people without their knowledge with nothing more than a push of the button on your iPhone. Just ask Donald Sterling, whose racist rants to his mistress, recorded in what was presumably the privacy of his own home, cost him ownership of the Los Angeles Clippers basketball team (and his marriage as well—his fed-up wife of fifty years filed for divorce).

The other great shift that took place in recent years was the move toward working more from home. Many CEOs and executives maintain full home offices. When a corporate executive calls me to check in about monitoring their office space, I always ask, "What about your home . . . do you ever talk business from home?" Let's take, for example, a research and development executive at a Fortune 500 company. These guys are natural targets.

"Sure, all the time, we even hold meetings and parties sometimes; I have a home office there." I then tell them about the need for bug sweeps. I also remind them that it's usually much easier to tap their phones at home instead of at work. Another way we get business is when executives have help in to set up their home offices. The general public has become much more aware of cybercrimes and hacking and the need to keep communications as secure as possible. The computer techs who set up their systems and firewalls may inquire about other security measures, including cameras or phone lines. Then they give us a call, because we are known to have the necessary equipment to do the job. We have the technical knowledge to do a two-day, three-phase sweep, and we have the equipment. I have invested in three sets of extremely complicated, large, and expensive equipment and retained the best technicians in the country.

In recent years, starting in 2016, there has been a dramatic rise in the call for bug sweeps at personal residences. The vast majority of the time, when we find bugs in the home, it's a device planted in the bedroom of a soon-to-be-ex-wife during a nasty divorce. The hubby is a control freak who wants to keep tabs on who she's sleeping with now that he's out of the house. The bugging device has the added advantage of allowing him to hear all her strategies about the divorce and monitor her conversations, so he can maintain the upper hand during the process.

Being "bugged" is an area where we tread lightly with our clients, as "bugging" tends to bring out some people with highly paranoid tendencies. However, it is a fact that out of all the home sweeps we do, we find some sort of bug in 16–17 percent of the cases . . . a not insignificant number! Below are some warning signs that your home might be bugged:

- Unusual static or beeps from your phone receiver or headset
- Crackling on your phone lines
- The feeling that someone has been inside your home
- People know more about your life or schedule than they should
- Your television is not clear
- Electrical panels have been tampered with
- Discoloration and dust from drilling in walls or ceilings
- New items (clocks, pens, and the like) you didn't order are delivered
- Repairmen appear to do jobs you weren't aware of

Most private investigators in the United States are *not* trained or experts in this subject matter, so let me lay it out for you. In terms of cost, a full sweep of an average-sized home of 3,000 square feet or less costs approximately $4,800. A dollar-fifty per square foot is a good average figure to go by for those residences over 3,000 square feet. Unfortunately, many investigators pretend to "sweep" a home or business for camera and monitoring devices by waving a "magic wand" purchased at

Radio Shack. Beware, you are being ripped off. A professional bug sweep includes the use of physical and visual inspections and state-of-the-art, current, counter-surveillance equipment. Your privacy and security is a serious matter, so please make sure you get someone who knows what they are doing!

* * *

Your home is most likely the biggest purchase you will make and by far the most valuable asset you will own in your lifetime. In my work as an investigator, I have seen hundreds of families torn apart due to inheritance issues. There is no fight as bitter as a family fight, and tempers tend to flare over money/property or disputes about health care decisions for an aging parent. I urge everyone to avoid these rifts at all costs. Clearly and legally, lay out exactly how you want your earthly goods disposed of and how your health care will be administered.

As I was working on this chapter of the book, news emerged that musical legend Prince, whose sudden death shocked the world, died intestate—without a will. I was surprised to hear this. Prince had access to the highest-level advisors and legal teams, who most certainly urged him over the years to do so. He had at one point married and fathered a child and in the last years of his life suffered from poor health—times when most people make out a will if they haven't already. Not to mention that he was a man very much in control of his affairs and image. It's hard to believe he didn't have strong feelings about the disposition of his fortune, estate, and most especially his studio and musical library.

Mostly, I was surprised because Prince was nothing if not brilliant, and not having a will is just a dumb move. That goes for him, that goes for all rich people, and that goes for average citizens who own a small house, old car, and work a regular job. For years, I harped on family, friends, and clients to at least make out a simple will. In recent years, I changed my mind. I now advocate a revocable living trust (RLT). Trusts are not just for millionaires. They're a great financial tool for most middle-class citizens.

But let's back up a moment and review. It is important to understand the three main documents that you should definitely consider. A will is a piece of paper that legally declares where your assets go upon your death, and having one is better than having nothing at all. The downside is that a will benefits the sitting judge at the courthouse, not any of your relatives or heirs. Did you know that 15–20 percent of your money goes to the county in probate fees when you die?

Anyone with more than a hundred thousand dollars in assets should establish a trust. I don't mean do-it-yourself with a form online, but hiring a first-rate attorney who specializes in wills and trusts.

A revocable living trust, so-called because you make and change them along with your circumstances during your lifetime, also determines who inherits your assets when you die. I estimate that establishing a trust will cost you between twenty-five hundred to four thousand dollars. In the long run, that will save your estate and beneficiaries the previously referenced fifteen to twenty percent in fees. If you have a million dollars in assets and die without a will, a lawyer will be appointed in your county to probate your will. He will get paid, and the county will get approximately $150,000 to $200,000 of your hard-earned money.

Finally, when you establish a medical power of attorney, aka "durable power of attorney for health care," you have officially designated a trusted family member or friend to make health care decisions if and when you are unable to do so. I cannot recommend strongly enough that everyone take the time to assign someone to do this for you.

Do some research and planning while you are still alive. Do your best now to ensure that your wishes about your health are followed in the last days of your life and that, once you are gone, the person or persons who inherit your home receive a wonderful, trouble-free inheritance.

I find estate planning to be a fascinating branch of the law, one I have been practicing for twenty-six years. The firm I founded is well known for handling some of the largest and most complex estates in California. However, when it comes to family matters, the issues are the same at every income level. It is the average-income person who stands to lose the most from a lack of planning. Whether it's due to taxes or legal fees, problems or expenses that arise from settling the estate, any loss can be punishing for their heirs. I cannot overstate how important preparing for this eventuality is for every family.

To cover the basics, a will and a trust are very different tools. A *will* is a set of written instructions for one person: the probate judge. That judge will dictate every single step of what bills are paid, how monies are distributed, and what happens throughout the entire process after you die. A *trust* allows you to designate one person (or co-trustees) to be in charge and dictate how the estate is handled and the assets distributed. After your death, this person is automatically authorized to handle tasks directly with the financial institutions; they do not require the probate court to supervise any step, unless the court's help is requested.

The overriding reason people execute wills and trusts is to take care of their families. They want to ensure that the surviving spouse and/or children are able to carry on upon their death. The last thing anyone wants is for family members to encounter delays, restrictions, or red tape when it comes to accessing the money and property they are leaving behind. This becomes particularly important for families with a disabled beneficiary. Needs-based benefits for disabled individuals are based on a financial eligibility process. If you have a spouse or child who receives disability benefits, inheriting money or property might cause these benefits to be cut off.

Special needs trusts are an extremely specialized field. At our firm, we work with many fine personal injury attorneys who are helping families win a settlement or award in the case of an accident or malpractice. We also work closely with NAMI, the National Alliance on Mental Illness, advocates for those suffering from mental illness. They are an invaluable resource when it comes to guiding caretakers to support and financial options for a family member disabled by mental issues.

If you have a disabled spouse or child and fail to arrange for a plan after you're gone, you have now magnified the damage. Not only did you fail to properly arrange for your house and/or other assets to be there for them, you've also probably disqualified them from their benefits—at least for a time. And with their primary caretaker gone, who will advocate to get those benefits back? No matter what your family situation, if you haven't gone to speak to an estate lawyer about such matters, the time is now.

It is critical that you consult with a reputable estate lawyer about your situation. A handwritten letter of instructions does not take the place of a will or trust. The only thing it does is create enormous expense with the probate court. Such a document invites various lawyers to weigh in with multiple interpretations of your words. What you thought was perfectly clear when writing out instructions may, but more likely will not, comply with the many sections of the probate code. No matter how well-meaning you are or how well-written your letter, handwritten stipulations nearly always fail to comply with the legal requirements for a will. A letter or fill-in-the-blank form you find online is an invitation to delay, dispute, expense, and disaster.

You will not be the exception to this rule. Oftentimes people seem to believe that estate laws apply to everybody else, but not to them. That's simply not true. Laws are in place, and they cover you whether you are aware of them or not. Ignorance is not bliss; it's in your best interests to visit an attorney to make sure that you protect yourself and your heirs. If you leave it up to the probate court, they will make a public display of the mess you left behind. Worse, without proper instruction, much of your estate will be depleted and only leftovers distributed.

Jillyn Hess-Verdon

Founder and Managing Partner

Hess-Verdon and Associates, PLC

10

INTERNATIONAL INCIDENTS

There are very few places on this globe a person might find him- or herself needing help where I haven't actually had some work experience. Having served the Department of Justice in more than sixty countries and investigated or vacationed in sixty more, I understand the way things work in many far-flung, disparate destinations.

I quickly learned that the American embassy in every foreign country is laid out exactly the same way. I can make sense of the whole alphabet soup of all those confusing three-letter agencies: ATF (Bureau of Alcohol, Tobacco, Firearms and Explosives), DEA (Drug Enforcement Administration), FBI (Federal Bureau of Investigation), and AID (code for CIA—they're secretive—you will never see "CIA" announced on a sign anywhere). I know how to reach the US ambassador and/or the chargé d'affaires, his or her second in command, the officials who have the most influence when it comes to protecting the rights of Americans in each particular country. I have at least a basic knowledge of the various justice codes and penal systems. This sort of experience can make all the difference should you find yourself in trouble in a foreign country.

There is never a shortage of Americans finding trouble abroad—frequently due to their own bad behavior. In 2015, a young University of Virginia student named Otto Warmbier made headlines when he was sentenced to fifteen years of hard labor in North Korea. He was convicted of stealing a promotional poster from his hotel. There was never any doubt he did it; he was captured on videotape taking it down from a wall. It came out at Otto's trial that someone from his church group at home put him up to getting a "souvenir" of his trip.

There is no doubt that this young man was highly intelligent, or at least book smart enough to gain admission to a prestigious university. Unfortunately, he was sadly lacking in street smarts and travel sense. Did he really not do any reading about the country he planned to visit? Did he never notice the security cameras following his every move in this most restrictive of all countries? American officials immediately and strongly denounced his brutal sentence and began a campaign to secure his release.

Throughout my travels, I have seen every possible variation of the "ugly American" in every country I visited. I am a big believer in seeing the world and encourage people of all ages to travel widely. However, I urge travelers young and old to have some humility. Follow the rules. Be a good guest. The fate of Otto Warmbier is a stark reminder of what can happen when you don't! Too many foreign countries relish the chance to teach Americans a harsh lesson when they are handed the opportunity.

I have visited unfortunates locked up in prisons all over the world. Believe me when I say that *Locked Up Abroad* is a fairy tale compared to the real-life conditions I've seen in, say, a Turkish, Thai, or Brazilian prison. I actually spent time living and working in Bogotá, Colombia; Quito, Ecuador; and Caracas, Venezuela. Paraguay, Uruguay, and Chile as well. I witnessed firsthand the abject poverty so rampant in many areas of these countries. For many dope peddlers, the drug trade was the one possible brass ring they had to reach for. I have softened a bit since my years as an agent in the DEA; I can understand and sympathize with young people who have no hope of ever making more than a dollar a day, if that. To reach for the riches that are possible in the drug trade is their best and only option. These people have very little to lose.

It is much more difficult for me to understand the combination of greed and naïveté that drives regular, middle-class Americans and other Westerners to smuggle drugs. Trust me, when I was stationed at Los Angeles International Airport I saw every trick in the book, including an actual nun who smuggled cocaine under her voluminous habit. She went to prison for twenty-five years. She served her time in America, fortunately, where the worst prisons are like Holiday Inns compared to prisons overseas. I've seen six to eight men held in a cell meant for two, just for starters. The inhumanity is hard for Americans to imagine. Believe me, the worst puppy mill in this country treats their animals better than many countries treat their human prisoners. Several places I visited scared the crap out of me, and I had a gun, badge, credentials, and the American government on my side.

It is likely you will serve hard time should you be absolutely crazy enough to get involved with drugs in a foreign country. That's if you're lucky. Indonesian authorities executed eight men and women, including the twenty-two- and twenty-four-year old Australian ringleaders, for drug smuggling as recently as 2015. It should go without saying, but don't do drugs in a foreign country, much less think for a second of transporting or smuggling them. There is absolutely no reason to resort to such desperately dangerous measures.

As a government employee, I was fortunate enough to be given briefings by the State Department on customs and cultures of the countries we visited for work. If you have an adventurous bent, the onus is on you to do your research. If you must backpack in Afghanistan or tour North Korea for fun, do your homework. Remember, you are not pulling pranks at a frat house in Virginia, so please act accordingly.

❊ ❊ ❊

Some years ago, I was traveling through Turkey with my wife and two other couples as part of a large tour group. On our last day in Ankara, we made sure to be outside lined up and ready to go on time, as we absolutely had to be at the airport several hours before our flight left for Istanbul. The tour director had just finished a final head count of passengers when the tour manager, accompanied by uniformed police officers, boarded the bus and announced that one of the guests had stolen the small plastic shoehorn from their room.

"Whoever stole the shoehorn, announce yourself and turn it in now!" No one moved. "Do it now, or we will search every passenger and piece of luggage on this bus until we find it!"

Given my past experience, I hoped that I could defuse the situation a bit. It was a lot of drama for a small piece of plastic that could not be worth more than a dime. I raised my hand. "Did you steal the shoehorn?" the tour manager demanded. I rose to my feet.

"No, I did not, but I understand you are upset, and rightly so. Could I pay you for the cost of the missing shoehorn, so you don't have to go to all this trouble?"

"Sir. Sit down and shut up, immediately." OK, OK, got it. I sat. My wife gave me a dirty look for my trouble. The authorities were going to find that shoehorn. Our bus wasn't moving.

Miraculously, the missing shoehorn quickly "appeared" on an empty seat, though no one claimed responsibility. After a long conference, it was decided that the police did not need to investigate the matter further and we could proceed to the airport. We all breathed a sigh of relief as the door shut behind the officers, the bus pulled into traffic, and we continued on our journey.

INTERNATIONAL ADOPTION

In 2010 long-simmering tensions between the U.S. and Russia concerning international adoptions exploded when a Tennessee mother placed the son she had adopted from a grim Siberian orphanage on a plane. He flew unaccompanied on a ten-hour ride back to his homeland. The boy carried a note addressed "To Whom It May Concern." In part, it read: "This child is mentally unstable . . . violent and has severe psychopathic issues/behaviors . . . I no longer wish to parent this child . . . and would like the adoption disannulled."

Russian authorities reacted with outrage, blasting the adoptive mother, who happened to be a registered nurse and the mother of another biological son. As officials at the highest levels in both countries investigated, they heard two very different stories. The mother claimed that the boy, who had lived with his alcoholic birth mother until she relinquished custody when he was six, was violent and unstable, and she literally feared for her life after he repeatedly threatened to burn her house down. She accused the orphanage of misleading her about the boy's mental stability, saying that staffers downplayed the severity of his problems in order to get him out of their facility.

Russian officials strongly denied these charges. Workers at the adoption agency said the child was completely normal for his age apart from being a bit stubborn. They also pointed out the woman had spent four days with the boy at the orphanage before being allowed to adopt him and in follow-up checks had never said anything was amiss. This "return" was the last straw after several other incidents, including one in which an adopted Russian child died when left outside in a car in freezing cold Midwest winter temperatures. The Russian foreign minister called for a ban on foreign adoptions to the United States . . . which soon enough came to pass.

That notorious case perfectly illustrates just one of the reasons why throughout my entire career I have strongly cautioned clients seeking to adopt internationally. In fact, I do my best to steer people away from the idea entirely. I understand that there are many happy American families whose child was adopted from a foreign country. To speak out against the practice is painting with a broad brush, I realize, but I do it because I have seen so many scams over the years. There are just too many people and places out there claiming to specialize in international adoptions that are crooks. Plenty of money flows in, but the promised child never arrives.

By the time my clients come to me broaching the idea of foreign adoption, they've generally spent the past five to ten years undergoing all kinds of painful, invasive, and expensive fertility treatments . . . all in vain. Sometimes they have also spent time exploring domestic adoption, which for one reason or another has proven prohibitive. They're already out a small fortune, getting older every day, and more anxious than ever for a child. They'll pay anything, go anywhere, do anything. That makes them an easy mark.

I empathize with the human desire—no, need—for a child. But this atmosphere breeds fly-by-night businesses run by con artists. Too many con artists will take your money and break your heart, and in the end, you will be out a lot of money and still not have a child. The ABC Adoption Agency operates for a while, scams some sincere wannabe parents, gets investigated, closes down, and vanishes, then reopens the next month with a new number and website called the XYZ Agency.

People get so warm and fuzzy. By adopting, not only will they fulfill their lifetime dream of becoming a parent, they're going to save a child from poverty and a destitute life as an orphan. It sounds good; the reality is different. Have you ever even traveled as a tourist to the country where you hope to get a child? I've spent significant time in all the most popular places for Americans to adopt internationally. Trust me, the process is grueling. Just to get visa to visit China or Africa is a hassle; you could gain entrance to the White House more easily. And now you want to try to get a child out?

I realize that this may come off as harsh and cynical, and I don't mean to sound that way. I do want to make readers aware that there are some highly unscrupulous people in America who will make all kinds of promises and take vast sums of money to arrange an overseas adoption before vanishing without a trace, never to be seen again. There are equally heartless workers in foreign countries who have absolutely zero compunctions about fobbing babies and children with serious physical, mental, or emotional difficulties off on Americans who are dying to become parents—and charging them a huge price for the privilege.

Let me make myself clear: I am not talking about those parents who willingly take on special-needs children. I am talking about would-be parents being absolutely and utterly deceived about everything from where the child was born to who the parents were, to what his or her early life was like. I am talking about children who are spiritually and academically compromised, saddled with lifelong conditions like fetal alcohol syndrome or reactive attachment disorder.

So what alternative would I offer? It's a bit like when a client contemplating divorce comes to me and says, "I know my spouse is hiding assets overseas. He fishes in the Bahamas. He's hidden money there, or someplace! I'm sure of it!" I generally ask, "Should we not begin our search here, in your home state, and then search all US banks before we undertake a search for offshore accounts in every random Caribbean island? Wouldn't it be simpler and more logical to at least start closer to home?"

When adopting a child, I highly recommend that you start or revisit your quest in the United States. That way you can easily travel to Los Angeles or Dallas or New York and visit the agency or attorney in person to ask the three big questions: 1) What is the adoption plan to get us a child? 2) How long will it take for me/us to adopt a child? 3) How much will this process cost? If you start with those three questions, you'll be light-years ahead of 75 percent of those beginning the journey.

As always, you have to do your homework.

* * *

Stashing money in offshore accounts and shady tax havens is standard practice for the world's richest people and corporations. A study conducted by James Henry of McKinsey and Company in 2012 found that that the wealthiest citizens have secreted more than $21 trillion in offshore accounts.[1] The rich, famous, and infamous are caught engaging in such illegal financial shenanigans with depressing regularity.

In 2012, Jerome Cahuzac was appointed Budget Minister of France. His job was to help the socialist President Hollande in his sworn mission to force their country's rich to pay their fair share of taxes and expose French tax avoiders. Only a year into his new post, the hugely wealthy former plastic surgeon was forced to resign. After months of the strongest possible denials, he admitted he had for decades concealed major assets in Switzerland and then Singapore. Cahuzac's wife, whom he was in the midst of divorcing, swore he had millions stashed in the Isle of Man as well. This was a particularly egregious example of hypocrisy, but the problem is hardly limited to France.

Several years later, the financial press around the world exploded when a huge trove of documents was leaked from Mossack Fonseca, a Panamanian law firm whose dealings were shrouded in secrecy. The information contained in what became known as "The Panama Papers" was nothing short of devastating. As the BBC reported, the documents implicated twelve current or former heads of state and government, including dictators accused of looting their own countries, in addition to more than sixty relatives and associates of heads of state.

The explosive scandal touched every corner of the globe. The papers implicated known close associates of Russian President Vladimir Putin in a suspected billion-dollar money-laundering ring. The UK's Prime Minister David Cameron was forced to defend details of the family trust set up by his father. When details of his wealthy wife's financial arrangements were leaked, Iceland's prime minister was forced to resign. All told, the papers revealed that more than 500 banks serving clients from Barcelona to China and Pakistan to Uruguay had set up more than 15,000 shell companies using Mossack Fonseca.

Right here in Orange County, USA, I am no stranger to domestic and foreign asset searches. This is simply standard operating procedure when I work divorce cases. However, offshore accounts are far from the

---

1. "Exhaustive Study Finds Global Elite Hiding Up To $32 Trillion in Offshore Accounts," July 31, 2012,http://www.m.democracynow.org/stories/12963.

only way to hide significant assets. Over the years, I have seen men and women try to hide assets in many ways, including:

- Putting assets under the names of family members
- Hiding businesses under illegal names
- Converting cash into large items like cars, boats, or even planes
- Converting cash into small items like diamonds, which are easily hidden and transported
- Storing cash in safety deposit boxes under false names in distant cities
- Giving "gifts" to family members or friends

Thanks to ever-evolving technologies and the increasing number of loopholes available, people and corporations are now able to get more creative than ever in the ways that they are able to hide away their assets. If you believe that your significant other is hiding assets, you might be tempted to use asset search services that you find online. As previously discussed, there are many forms of data freely available to the public to help you determine who owns what.

Remember, however, that you get what you pay for. These services do not come with actual private investigators who will explore the many diverse avenues that can be taken to squirrel away assets both here and abroad. Not only will these databases likely be missing important information, the information that is available may not be admissible in court.

At Martin Investigative Services, we perform several kinds of searches. They are not inexpensive. Beware of information brokers or so-called investigators who offer to run these searches for $500 or less. That is simply a come-on, and assets are very rarely ever found by them.

A basic asset/background search for a US resident or company costs $950.00 and takes twenty-four hours to turnaround. It includes but is not limited to the following:

- Twenty-year address history
- Obtaining/confirming subject's Social Security and date of birth
- Name of anyone using their Social Security number, including addresses
- All statewide real property
- Consumer public filings nationwide: includes bankruptcies, notice of defaults, judgments, tax liens, and problems with the IRS

- Corporate and limited financial partnership information
- Civil and criminal (felony and misdemeanor) records in fifteen of the fifty-eight California counties
- Fictitious business name index
- Professional licensing
- Names and addresses of neighbors and businesses

The basic search does not include bank, savings, or checking accounts or stocks, bonds, and securities. So where's the beef? The real meat? There are two options. A bank, savings, and checking account search costs $4,800 per state, $7,500 nationwide, with turnaround of five to eight working days. A stocks, bonds, and securities search likewise costs $4,800 per state, $7,500 nationwide, and takes five to eight working days. This kind of work is a real specialty, and you need to retain an investigator who specializes in that kind of work to handle it for you.

Oh, many private investigators *claim* to do complete financial asset searches, but a search for bank account records and stocks, bonds, and securities is a completely different matter. Your investigator must be able to locate these hidden assets legally. Without proper documentation, you won't be able to take a writ of attachment down to the bank and get money you are owed in a judgment . . . or prevail in divorce court.

What's most important to know about asset searches is that a sea change took place when President Bill Clinton signed the Gramm-Leach-Bliley Act into law back in 1999. Among other provisions, the act was meant to protect consumers by making sure there was a valid, lawful reason to go digging in someone's financial records. The act prohibits subterfuge, random running of credit reports, gagging people at banks, and pretending to be someone else in order to get bank information. At the turn of the century, there were probably 200 companies who did full bank asset searches. Now it's down to about five who are really equipped to do it—legally.

As we discussed back in chapter 4, let's say you're dating somebody and are curious about his financial picture . . . or your child is thinking about getting married. There's no problem running a basic asset search on them. But you cannot do a bank search just because you're curious. The penalties for this kind of snooping are stiff, including fines and jail time. That's why you need an ethical investigator who knows what he's doing.

Finally, a word about foreign asset searches. We take them on a case-by-case basis on a per-country rate. Should we locate foreign assets, we petition that bank and bring the money back to the United States. There are countries, however, who refuse to send money back even if it is found, and we go through every legal channel possible. If your estranged spouse has hidden money in Switzerland, we can probably get it back. Luxembourg, no. Even legal writs and letters from the IRS won't convince them.

Here's the really interesting fact that I've noticed from decades of experience doing extensive asset searches: most rich people are control freaks who have no desire to stash their money overseas. There are too many complications. I would estimate that 95 percent of Americans keep all their money within thirty miles of their home address. It is truly the 1 percent who have the desire and know-how to hide money in foreign countries; the rest figure out a way to hide it closer to home. Secret Swiss accounts are not as common as people would think in real life, though headlines, novels, and movies make it seem almost commonplace.

Make sure your investigator has the necessary experience and know-how when it comes to identifying hidden accounts and other secret assets. Make sure they are also fully compliant with the GLB Act and the Fair Credit Reporting Act. If the potential investigator does not mention these two items, do not hire them. The information you need is out there and can be found; just make sure you obtain it and use it in the right way.

Hopefully, you will never have to retain a private investigator while doing business or vacationing abroad. Unfortunately, when the need for such services arises, it is usually due to some sort of crisis or emergency. There simply isn't time to screen a PI like you would do at home.

Foreign PIs usually offer the same services and conduct investigations similar to those of their US counterparts, but far from home, how do you ensure that you are hiring a legitimate professional? This task is made more difficult when the local laws for PIs are not even clear. If you fall victim to a scammer, not only will you receive no help, but the best-case scenario might be that you lose your retainer. Worst case, your valuable, sensitive personal information will have fallen into the wrong hands.

Let's say you need a PI in Mexico, my country—a very popular destination for Americans. Google will show several nice websites, but how do you pick a real and professional PI to assist you in Mexico? Usually a normal person contacts two or three websites and hires the PI that "seems the most legitimate." Big mistake. The best crooks in the world are the ones who tell you exactly what you want to hear. I know of several cases where foreign clients were scammed or even extorted by a virtual PI "found on the Internet."

Doing some due diligence before you make a hiring decision will pay off in the long run. Here are my five best tips to consider before hiring a PI abroad (in no particular order of importance):

1. Ask for References and Referrals

A good PI should always provide you with references or testimonials. If you do not want to directly ask the PI, you can always call home to ask your local or national PI association for a referral. You might also consider reaching out to your attorney—they usually know how to get good referrals from other colleagues.

2. Find Out Who Regulates the Industry in That Country and Make Sure the PI You Want to Hire Is Licensed and/or His Business Is Legit

This could be a bit tricky, but the Internet can be of great help in this task. You may call the association's licensing body to find out if there have been any complaints filed on the investigator, or check to see that he's actually licensed, for starters. Sometimes you can find licensing details on their company website, making it easier to verify credentials. Whatever it takes, do it.

3. Professional Certifications and Affiliations

Going one step further, check out the website of the PI you are considering and review his résumé, experience, and services. A good PI will absolutely display his professional certifications and affiliations. And don't just believe everything you see—you need to check these too. Go to the website of the association where the PI claims to be a member and check to see that he is listed in their directory. Or call them and confirm he is a member in good standing. This caution beforehand is well worth it in the long run.

4. Communication

You've sent an e-mail outlining your problem and the PI has not answered 24–36 hours later. Keep on looking. The lack of prompt, clear communication is always an early symptom of a bad service provider. Of course, every case and client is different, but a good PI will respond to your initial inquiry in a timely manner and keep in contact every two or three days until the investigation is completed.

5. Assume Nothing

Make sure the PI understands exactly what it is you want accomplished. Make sure that you know exactly how much you will be paying for the investigation and how the reports are going to be delivered and when. Sometimes a flat fee will be established, but if you are going to be charged by the hour make sure to know a minimum and a maximum of hours to be charged depending on the case. An NDA (nondisclosure agreement) is a must when your PI will be handling sensitive information.

A good final report will contain a narrative of the investigation, video prints, photographs, DVDs, criminal or civil records, social media pictures, and more depending on the type of investigation undertaken.

Following these five tips will ensure that your experience with a foreign PI is both positive and productive. Wishing you happy and safe travels throughout the world.

Fernando Molina

Senior Investigator—Mexico

Martin Investigative Services

11

THE ETHICS OF INVESTIGATING

How to Hire the Right PI

PRIVATE INVESTIGATOR

Do you enjoy unraveling riddles or solving puzzles? Are you a detail-oriented individual? You probably are a good candidate for our next Private Investigator class (June 6–June 12).

At xxxx Training Academy we provide you with the most comprehensive Private Investigator training anywhere in the State. Our experienced instructors go above and beyond the minimum standards required by the Department of Criminal Justice Services to certify you as a Private Investigator. We will also assist you in submitting your registration documents to the Department of Criminal Justice Services when you complete our course so you can receive your Credentials as quickly as possible. We also actively assist you with Job Placement opportunities upon your becoming certified with DCJS.

Because this is a very competitive Career Field and seats in our classes are limited to ten (10) candidates only, we do have an interview process. Please call xxx to schedule an interview in order to reserve yourself a seat in the next class. We look forward to meeting with you.

This is an actual ad[1] that ran recently in various cities nationwide on several employment sites. For those of you who are interested in private investigation as a career, let me offer a warning: You can't go to school to become a PI. When I worked out of my office in the shopping center in Orange County, one of those "technical colleges" that offered classes in all sorts of fields had a "campus" just across the street. One of the courses they offered was "How to Become a Private Investigator." Those poor students . . . a few of them came over to my office, proudly waving their diploma in front of me, inquiring about work opportunities. I would say, politely, "Let me be frank. That diploma is worthless. It is of no value in the private investigative establishment."

The school instructors came over more than once to ask if I wanted to teach, but I always turned them down flat. I wasn't willing to mislead the students in that way, even though the easy money was tempting. I strongly urge anyone who is thinking about taking some sort of course in private investigation to ask the school these questions: "How many people graduated from your last class, and where are they now employed as investigators, if anywhere?" Once, on a radio show, I got so sick of hearing about these "degrees" that I said, "I will give someone ten thousand dollars cash if they can prove to me that a course they took helped them pass the test to obtain their license." I required that the claimant would show their valid license, of course. The phone never rang; I knew it wouldn't.

To return to the above ad. I called the number provided and spoke to the woman representing the school. I learned that this particular course cost $795, though I know of some people who have paid up to ten thousand dollars for "special training." I then asked, "Do I have to sit for my PI license test after taking this course, or will I automatically be qualified and licensed if I pass?"

"We will help you with all that," she assured me. Despite my pressing her, that was as specific as she would get. She did urge me, several times, to come to the office for my in-person evaluation, as space was extremely limited.

Just in case you haven't gotten the message yet: if you attend a PI school, online or in person, after you've paid your fees and done the required coursework, you will not be the slightest bit closer to getting

---

1. From the Norfolk Craigslist "legal/paralegal" jobs page; the listing has since expired.

your license. Whatever state you live in, you must call the bureau that licenses private investigators. A simple online search of "private investigator licensing in Alabama," for example, should start you on your way. Obviously, skip all those ads that show up first for schools like I'm talking about, because they are numerous and they are prominently placed.

The information packet you will receive, for free, outlines your state's criteria to become a licensed private investigator. Your state may require two thousand hours of experience, which equals one year of work as an investigator. The requirement could be up to six thousand hours, or three years of work experience, before you can sit for your license. Sometimes a combination of work experience and college-level coursework are accepted; every state is different. In California, for example, the rules are particularly tough. Six thousand hours of work experience is required, and that means hours certified by a superior and backed up by paystubs and tax returns.

Working as a police officer or in various law enforcement agencies will qualify as "investigative" work. Working at a PI agency could also qualify in many cases, though it's nearly impossible to get a job without a license. I'm not willing to train my own grandson to become a private investigator, and I would dearly love for him to get into this business. It would simply take too much time and effort for me to try to teach him all he needs to know, when I have top-notch former FBI, CIA, DEA, and Secret Service agents applying for work at my company at the rate of nearly one per day.

For young people who want to be private eyes, here's the bottom line. Start with a five-year plan, which begins with getting a criminal justice degree and then going into law enforcement, preferably at the federal level. Learn how to conduct surveillance. Become proficient at taking an official statement. Get lots of practice interviewing and interrogating suspects. Hone your instincts for identifying suspicious behavior. Get comfortable testifying in court. Understand how the justice system really works. And listen, don't even approach me about a job until you're thirty-five. Until then, you don't have enough life experience.

Also, somewhere along the way, develop your own style. Friendly, low-key, easygoing . . . the "good guy" who lulls people into confessing or telling all. Or full-on frightening: scaring and intimidating people into spilling the beans. This persona will come with time. As I've discussed throughout this book, the PI business has changed radically over the years, but the cornerstone is and has always been interview and interrogation. Anyone can follow someone around and do a surveillance; that doesn't require a tremendous skill set. Being a top-notch investigator requires skills that cannot be easily taught; only time and plenty of experience will bring them out.

And by the way . . . ladies? I am looking for you! I was only the second agent in the country to have a female partner when I worked in the Department of Justice. And I will be honest, taking on my new partner was not a prospect that thrilled me. We were macho drug enforcement agents, kicking ass and taking names. What, exactly, was I going to do with this girl? Then I saw her in action on an undercover drug buy, where a dope peddler fell all over himself, incriminating himself and everybody else in an attempt to impress her. It dawned on me right then, along with all my male colleagues, that we had been missing out on a great resource.

Unfortunately, female private investigators are pretty thin on the ground. They probably make up less than 1 percent of licensed investigators in the private sector. Let me tell you, ladies, if you are a female Spanish speaker with a solid law enforcement background, there is no limit to how much money you could make in this business.

However, I understand it can seem a bit like trying to become a race-car driver . . . how are you going to win the race if no one will let you on the track? How are you going to become a movie star if you can't get a role without a SAG card, and can't get a SAG card without acting experience? I am in no way trying to discourage anybody; in fact, just the opposite. It's tough to become a good professional anything! It's not easy to become the president of the United States . . . but if you do, the perks are phenomenal. If you can get your license and are willing to work hard in your career as a private investigator, the sky is the limit!

❅ ❅ ❅

Speaking of PI schools, an old acquaintance of mine, I noticed one day, had come up with an online course he was advertising pretty heavily. He also sold all kinds of books, tests, and spy gear on his website. The next time I saw him, I asked him what in the world he was doing. He told me happily that he was making so much money from his school that he no longer had to work as an investigator. There's a sucker born every minute, and sometimes, I hate to say, PIs are the ones taking advantage. Some people say a PI's license is like a lawyer's license: license to steal.

However, the most common way private eyes take advantage of clients is to take a retainer and refuse to do any work. They sit back and hope the answer falls in their lap, more or less. Naturally, it usually doesn't, and they simply tell the client the person they followed didn't cheat, the missing person couldn't be located, or whatever lie is necessary. Sometimes they don't even bother to lie. Years ago, when I was the new kid on the block, there was a San Francisco guy around who was well known as the PI to the stars at that time. Then he took a $20,000 retainer from a client, didn't do the work, and simply refused to return the money. He just inexplicably dug in his heels. He lost his license over this; it was just foolish. These days he runs a sandwich shop.

Should you find yourself in that situation with a PI you've retained, don't hassle with small claims court or litigation. Report them to your state's licensing bureau; that will get their attention. There is nothing worse than taking a retainer and not doing the work. Certainly, there can be a legitimate dispute over work that was done, but when so-called "PIs" take a retainer and don't do anything, I encourage people to hit back, and threatening their license is the most effective way.

* * *

Of course, believing as I do that the right PI has the power to change lives for the better, I sincerely hope that you never encounter an unscrupulous investigator. I spoke a great deal at the beginning of this book about the importance of finding the right attorney, especially in family law matters. Finding the right PI is just as important.

The Internet is filled with private investigators who promise the world when it comes to civil, criminal, corporate, and insurance cases related to the public. It is ethical business practices, good character, and a sound reputation that separate good private investigators from those on every street corner. I absolutely encourage everyone to hire a PI to research important matters for them. However, you must do a bit of research yourself to find the right man (or woman).

Start by making sure the investigator is licensed and in good standing with the state where she/he is licensed. Another sign of credibility is when the investigator has an office as opposed to meeting clients in a coffee shop or bar. Having an office does not automatically make one a reputable private investigator, but it provides clients with a better measure of confidence and the ability to know they can return to a designated place if the wheels come off the investigation. This isn't an old movie. I don't know any reputable PIs who work out of bars.

While private investigators are not officially held to an attorney-client or doctor-patient level of confidentiality, a good one will honor this practice. Ensuring your privacy and best interests are attributes of an investigator with integrity and high standards of professionalism. Insist that your private investigator prepare any and all reports to your attorney of record to ensure the integrity of the attorney-client relationship. If you have no attorney of record, use the corporate attorney of record for the private investigation firm as an alternative.

It's critical to know the depth of the private investigator's experience. Education, law enforcement background, technical expertise, and years of professional practice, as well as a solid record of well-conducted cases, are important factors to note. For example, private investigators with a law enforcement or federal agent background know the system and how to work within its guidelines and procedures. They can produce evidence or other legal materials that will hold up in court. They are also prepared to testify in support of the evidence. Make sure the investigator you retain is considered an expert in the federal, state, or local court systems. If not, choose another investigative agency.

Selecting a private investigator by referral from a trusted friend is ideal. If this is not possible, you need to prepare a list of prospective private investigators. Law enforcement agencies can be contacted to refer recently retired officers who have established a solid track record as private investigators. Well-known attorneys, specializing in the particular area of law you are engaging in, are also a dependable resource. Do not hesitate to contact the clerks of the court, bailiffs, and other court personnel to inquire about investigators they might use in the given legal situation you are facing.

* * *

I always prefer to hire former federal agents with spotless records, as this gives me at least some assurance of their ethics. Just as I was getting established as a private investigator, I worked seven or eight cases for the top criminal defense attorney in Orange County. Of course, his business was a fantastic opportunity for me at the time. This particular attorney had a brilliant legal mind; he was the man to see in Southern California back then when you were in trouble . . . and his clients were always in deep trouble. Murder kind of trouble.

There was rarely a question in our minds of whether or not our client had committed the crime. They had, most of the time, unquestionably committed the crimes of which they were accused. The issue facing us was: Could we get them off? For me as a young investigator that was hard to swallow—to sit at a table across from someone I knew was a murderer and try to help them. Not that they ever came right out and told me, of course, but sometimes a couple of incriminating words slipped out accidentally. Usually, there was simply such an overwhelming preponderance of evidence that a five-year-old could clearly see our client was guilty.

I was always sitting there in the courtroom when the jury came back. My stomach would clench as the foreman read the verdict. "Not guilty" caused me just as much of a jolt as "Guilty." It was the strangest feeling. I finally came to accept, after a number of cases where our clients were acquitted, that I had to look at this as just another aspect of doing my job. Our client had an attorney and investigator who had done their best. Perhaps the district attorney did not do their job or do it well enough. There's a fine line to this justification, of course, but I absolutely believe that everyone is entitled to a defense, and every client deserves my best efforts.

I had to draw the line after the case of a gangbanger who we got off on a murder case. This kid shot a rival in cold blood in an alley. The jury didn't buy the eyewitness testimony of a witness, so he got off scot-free. Less than three weeks later—twenty days, to be precise, I remember it to the day—he was back in jail. Taken in on another murder charge. His mother called me again looking to hire me. On the spot, I made up a new rule. "One get-out-of-jail-free card per person." I wasn't about to do this on a regular basis. The lawyer I worked with, by the way, was eventually disbarred—they nailed him for perjury. Many years later I was driving in Vegas and saw him running a hot dog stand on Sahara Boulevard. He recently passed . . . R.I.P.

* * *

I've mentioned that many private investigators simply cannot handle dealing with the general public. One reason is because a small but statistically significant portion of people seeking out PI services have obvious mental health issues. This becomes a particular factor when people are requesting bug-sweeping because they feel that they are being watched or their phones are tapped. When such a person comes to our office, we politely escort them to the elevator.

Most of these clients are asked two simple questions before we agree to perform any service:

- Are you under the care of a doctor?
- Do you think you ought to be?

If the answer to either one of these questions is "yes," it does not mean automatic elimination for using our services, but I for one am not willing to indulge those suffering from mental illness, even for a fat paycheck. Sometimes, however, it's not quite that clear-cut. A woman recently drove up to one of our offices in a brand-new car, looking very presentable. She had a great job as an administrative officer at a big company. She was married to an equally accomplished man; they lived together in a lovely home in a nice neighborhood. Everything looked great on paper, but she had a problem. She was convinced someone was following her. A car was trailing her, she was sure of it.

I told her to get a license plate on this car, and we would run it. She provided us with one, we tracked the person, and our client had no idea who the person was, much less any connection to her. She continued to insist that people were still following her; she couldn't provide us with another plate number or come up with a reason someone would have to follow her. Of course, we ruled out the husband or anyone at her work surveilling her. We were at a stalemate.

It is at this point we have to wonder what, exactly, is going on here. In a wealthy community like Orange County, we have had a few clients who got very caught up in the cloak-and-dagger aspects of having their very own PI on call. It becomes a spending addiction like any other . . . shopping, drugs, shoplifting . . . something to give them a small jolt of excitement. I once tried to dissuade one of these women with far too much money and not enough to do by saying, "We've raised our rates . . . surveillance is now $500 an hour." She replied, "That's awfully high, but go ahead." I knew something was wrong, nothing we could fix. I simply won't take advantage of these kinds of people.

While we're talking about delusions, let me address "Gang Stalking," a term that started popping up on the Internet with some regularity a few years ago. It refers to prolonged, intense, unlawful surveillance and harassment of a person who has been designated as a target by a government representative. Every single one of the thirty-eight re-quests we received to find a client's gang stalker last year was sincere, but not one had any basis in reality.

Initially, when this first became a trending topic, we would conduct countersurveillance on the client in order to determine who might be responsible for this type of harassment. Interestingly, in all the cases we took, we never saw even one person who was supposedly relentlessly targeting the client. The most common reaction to this finding was, "They must have known you were there and taken the day off."

Many claimed to be victims of harassment by horns, sirens, helicop-ters, and "infrared signals" (another popular term they found on the Internet). We encouraged all our clients to photograph or record video of any of these occurrences. On those rare instances where the client returned with some sort of "evidence," it turned out to be bogus, 100 percent of the time. Clients could rarely articulate what the motives of their tormentors might be. The sad part was seeing how these men and women were absolutely convinced there was a deep-seated conspiracy by the government, relatives, or people from another planet to stalk them physically, psychologically, and spiritually.

As former federal agents, we did our best to assure these clients that they were not remotely close to being on the law enforcement commu-nity radar. I explained to them that agents from just about any govern-ment agency these days are preoccupied with more pressing matters (such as preventing terrorism). I also tactfully mentioned that any per-sonal mental demons one has do not give rise to any type of law en-forcement or private investigative agency assistance. That assessment was never warmly received. Of course, we would say that; we must be part of the conspiracy. Eventually, I drew the line. Gang stalking cases simply have no place in our investigative workload. We will absolutely not take your money or waste your or our time.

However, there is an old saying: "Just because you're paranoid doesn't mean they're not out to get you." These days, marital surveillances are falling by the wayside and, I predict, will soon become a thing of the past. Given the state of electronics, old-time full-scale surveillance is simply not needed. Cell phone records, texts, e-mail, calendars, appointments . . . cheaters carelessly give up the game so easily. Men and women leave compromising photos right there on the tablet, like Gwen Stefani found out when she found naked snaps of the family nanny on the kids' iPad one day.

Who needs a PI? Now a wife just looks on her husband's iCalendar, notes the locations, and we can track him in twenty minutes. Recently, we followed a man for seven days, for a wife who was sure her husband was cheating on her with her best friend. He was a good boy. He even attended church services. When we turned up nothing, my client insisted that her husband must have been on to us. I guaranteed her that that was simply not the case. He had no idea anyone was following him; he drove so fast we could barely keep up with him. Now, our client might be paranoid . . . but the paranoid make up about 3 percent of our marital surveillance clients. Ninety-seven percent of those who think their spouse is cheating are right. Some days I think the other 3 percent could be right, too . . . we really did just choose the wrong week to follow their spouse.

In my work at one of Southern California's best-known and well-established firms I concentrate on three areas of law. The first is federal criminal defense, defending people who have been charged or indicted by the US government. Next is conducting internal investigations for companies. Finally, I practice civil litigation.

It's very common for large law firms to employ private investigators, and Manatt, Phelps, and Phillips is no exception. I am very selective about who I use, because a truly superb investigator is nothing less than my partner in developing the evidence necessary to win our case. One of my requirements is that my private investigator comes from a law enforcement background. When it comes to finding a lawyer, I always advocate for a former law enforcement attorney. In other words, if the DA is gunning for you, you should hire a defense lawyer who once served as a district attorney. If the feds are after you, you want to retain a former US attorney to represent you. The same rule holds true for investigators.

PIs who are former law enforcement agents know exactly what they're going up against, as they were once on the other side. As a team, both attorney and investigator have a window to what the other side is thinking, their strategy, and how they are most likely to present their case in court.

It is also absolutely essential that we hire an investigator who is truthful, accurate, and complete in the job they do. When we are defending someone against serious government charges, or investigating alleged misconduct at a company, we must have an accurate and complete work product to take into court. It's essential that the investigators on the defense side are equal to, if not better than, the very best the US government can pit against us. Hiring the right investigator is where we might gain an advantage over our opponent. Sometimes, when putting together a case, the government can be sloppy. On the defense side, we never have the luxury of being sloppy.

Conscientious, thorough, and honest: these are traits we seek in private investigators. Impartial is another. Let's say my client is a company that suspects there's been some sort of misconduct, and we need to hire an investigator to see what happened. In those cases, we are not always acting as an advocate; we're more neutral, and that's why we need an investigator who is scrupulously honest and doesn't shade results one way or another to please us. We need to present an accurate picture to the company: what happened, why it happened, and what to do going forward, and maybe ways to avoid such issues in the future. An impartial investigator is critical.

Finally, a key quality in an investigator is someone who has a lot of energy. I want someone who feels passionate about my case, someone who, like me, is lying awake at night considering and discarding possible defenses and strategies. Someone who is always thinking ahead to the next door to knock on, the next lead to follow. That means not only interviewing one person, but possibly identifying other witnesses after an interview who might then shed further light on the situation.

An investigator is so key because they are needed in any case involving witnesses. If someone is testifying against us, we want an investigator to paint us a full picture of their background long before our day in court. One thing private investigators can do for us these days is an in-depth search of social media. This report gives us a great candid portrait of anybody and a far better understanding of who this person really is, not just the words on a page from their deposition. If the witness is important, we want to dig deep. This is all in the interest of preparation—we don't want surprises.

It can be very frightening to have the full force and weight of the US government leveled against you, but people are acquitted of such charges every day. It absolutely can be done. One of the advantages you have on the defense side is that with the right client—one is who truly committed to hiring the best attorney and investigator and listening to them—we have the luxury of concentrating solely on this one case. Whereas the government prosecutors are often juggling numerous cases at all times. As I well know, having the right investigator on our side can mean the difference between winning and losing.

Kenneth Julian, Partner

Manatt, Phelps, and Phillips, LLP

Costa Mesa, California

Some of these anecdotes and realities about working as a private investigator sound a little cynical, and I'd like to turn that around a bit here at the end. Every job has its challenges; not every job has the potential to change lives. That's what a great investigator can do, and it's the most rewarding feeling imaginable. If you are drawn to this profession, take what I've said about what you need to do to heart and get going on your own career. There are so many people out there who need your help.

It took a legendary boxer to show me the importance of what I was doing for my clients: which is helping them to fight back in a smart, strategic way. Decades ago, as a young man, I attended a boxing exhibition featuring Muhammed Ali in South Central Los Angeles with a high school buddy, John Schroyer. At that racially charged time in our country's history—not so very long ago—we happened to be the only two Caucasians in the huge audience. We certainly stood out in the crowd.

At one point, the garrulous Ali motioned for John to enter the ring and do a little sparring. John is a large man, but no fool. He quickly held his hands up to indicate that he wanted no part of Ali. The venue erupted in laughter when Ali told John, "You're smarter than you look!" We enjoyed a virtuoso performance that night from one of the all-time greats. His best was yet to come.

The legendary Rumble in The Jungle was held several years later in Kinshasa, Zaire (now The Republic of Congo), and pitted challenger Ali against world heavyweight champion George Foreman. Oddsmakers gave Ali little to no chance against the much stronger and heavier-hitting Foreman. Foreman was twenty-five years old to Ali's thirty-two. Ali had also been noncompetitive during his three-and-a-half year suspension for refusal to comply with the draft prior to this fight.

It was in this historic fight that Ali unleashed his brilliant strategy. The "rope-a-dope" is performed by the boxer assuming a protective stance. In Ali's case, he basically laid against the ropes and absorbed blows for the first seven rounds as Foreman gave him a brutal beating. Ali believed that much of the force from the punches would be absorbed by the ropes' elasticity rather than his body. Ali's plan was to let Foreman punch himself out and become totally exhausted, thus becoming easy prey. How ahead of its time was that?

By the start of the eighth round, Foreman was a mere shadow of his former self. The throwing of so many fierce punches had taken its toll. Ali came off the ropes and pounced on Foreman with a devastating barrage of combinations, sending his foe crashing to the canvas. The fight was stopped by the referee, and Ali was crowned heavyweight champion of the world once again.

Most of my clients are facing overwhelming obstacles, and I like to share with them the rope-a-dope story. So many women have been spiritually, physically, mentally, and professionally "beaten down" by their spouse or significant other for years, sometimes decades. They know all too well the feeling of leaning on the ropes while getting pummeled by a heavyweight. It is with great relish that I tell them they, too, can have an eighth round.

I encourage my clients to adopt Ali's brilliant strategy. He showed how to fight back in a smart, strategic, and legal way. My clients need to stand up and (figuratively) throw that first punch into their spouse's nose. The mere thought of this event will send shock waves through the other party. Just like Foreman, who would rather beat you for seven rounds, when Ali started fighting back, Foreman psychologically and physically checked out.

The rope-a-dope analogy can be applied to men, women, and children in many different case scenarios. If there is a negative situation in your life, think about fighting back. But fight back in a smart, strategic, and lawful way. Don't do anything physical that could get you harmed or even arrested. Figure out the best way to stop the abuse, harassment, or the placing of you in an unfair position. Then hire a PI to help you.

You have been on the ropes long enough. It is time for you to fight back, take control, and knock out the problems others are causing in your life. This is what I tell my own clients, and my sincere wish for those seeking guidance in this book!

INDEX